D1172009

WITHDRAWN

WITHDRAWN

Seal of the State of West Virginia

CHRONOLOGY AND DOCUMENTARY
HANDBOOK OF THE
STATE OF
WEST VIRGINIA

ROBERT I. VEXLER

State Editor

WILLIAM F. SWINDLER

Series Editor

1978 OCEANA PUBLICATIONS, INC./Dobbs Ferry, New York

CALVIN T. RYAN LIBRARY
KEARNEY STATE COLLEGE
KEARNEY, NEBRASKA

Library of Congress Cataloging in Publication Data

Main entry under title:

Chronology and documentary handbook of the State of
  West Virginia.

  (Chronologies and documentary handbooks of the
States ; 47)
    Bibliography: p.
    Includes index.
    SUMMARY: Contains a chronology of events in
West Virginia from 1661 to 1977, biographical sketches
of prominent citizens, and selected documents pertinent
to West Virginia.
    1. West Virginia—History—Chronology.   2. West
Virginia—Biography.   3. West Virginia—History—Sources.
[1. West Virginia—History]   I. Vexler, Robert I.
II. Series.

ISBN 0-379-16173-7   78-21049

© Copyright 1979 by Oceana Publications, Inc.

All rights reserved. No part of this publication may be reproduced or transmitted in any
form or by any means, electronic or mechanical, including photocopy, recording,
xerography, or any information storage and retrieval system, without permission in
writing from the publisher.

Manufactured in the United States of America

TABLE OF CONTENTS

ACKNOWLEDGMENT

Special recognition should be accorded Melvin Hecker, whose research has made a valuable contribution to this volume.

Thanks to my wife, Francine, in appreciation of her help in the preparation of this work.

Thanks also to my children, David and Melissa, without whose patience and understanding I would have been unable to devote the considerable time necessary for completing the state chronology series.

I also wish to acknowledge the scholarly research grant given to me by Pace University. This greatly eased the technical preparation of this work.

Robert I. Vexler
Pace University

INTRODUCTION

This projected series of *Chronologies and Documentary Handbooks of the States* will ultimately comprise fifty separate volumes—one for each of the states of the Union. Each volume is intended to provide a concise ready reference to basic data on the state, and to serve as a starting point for more extended study as the individual user may require. Hopefully, it will be a guidebook for a better informed citizenry - students, civic and service organizations, professional and business personnel, and others.

The editorial plan for the *Handbook* series falls into six divisions: (1) a chronology of selected events in the history of the state; (2) a short biographical directory of the principal public officials, e.g., governors, Senators and Representatives; (3) a short biographical directory of prominent personalities of the state (for most states); (4) the first state constitution; (5) the text of some representative documents illustrating main currents in the political, economic, social or cultural history of the state; and (6) a selected bibliography for those seeking further or more detailed information. Most of the data found in the present volume, in fact, have been taken from one or another of these references.

The current constitutions of all fifty states, as well as the federal Constitution, are regularly kept up to date in the definitive collection maintained by the Legislative Drafting Research of Columbia University and published by the publisher of the present series of *Handbooks*. These texts are available in most major libraries under the title, *Constitutions of the United States: National and State,* in two volumes, with a companion volume, the *Index Digest of State Constitutions.*

Finally, the complete collection of documents illustrative of the constitutional development of each state, from colonial or territorial status up to the current constitution as found in the Columbia University collection, is being prepared for publication in a multi-volume series by the present series editor. Whereas the present series of *Handbooks* is intended for a wide range of interested citizens, the series of annotated constitutional materials in the volumes of *Sources and Documents of U.S. Constitutions* is primarily for the specialist in government, history or law. This is not to suggest that the general citizenry may not profit equally from referring to these materials; rather it points up the separate purpose of the *Handbooks*, which is to guide the user of these and other sources of authoritative information with which he may systematically enrich his knowledge of this state and its place in the American Union.

William J. Swindler
John Marshall Professor of Law
College of William and Mary
Series Editor

Robert I. Vexler
Associate Professor of History
Pace University
Series Associate Editor

Montani Semper Liberi/
Mountaineers Are Always Free
State Motto

CHRONOLOGY

1661   King Charles II of Great Britain granted the land between the Potomac and Rappahannock rivers, the "Northern Neck," to a group of gentlemen. It was eventually granted to Thomas, Lord Fairfax.

1671   Under orders from Governor William Berkeley, General Abram Wood sent out an exploring party which discovered Kanawha Falls.

1716   Governor Alexander Spottswood and about 30 men traveled into the area known as Pendelton County.

1725   John Van Nehne, an Indian trader, went into the northern part of the state.

1726   Morgan Morgan, a Welshman, the first settler in what is now West Virginia erected a cabin at Bunker Hill.

1727   German settlers, who came to the region from Pennsylvania, established the town of New Mechlenburg, later Shepherdstown, on the Potomac River.

1742   John P. Sulley discovered coal on the Coal River.

1748   Harpers Ferry began carrying passengers across the Shenandoah River.

           George Washington surveyed part of the "Northern Neck."

1751   Christopher Gist, surveyor for the first Ohio Company, explored the area along the Ohio River north of the mouth of the Kanawha River.

           George Washington surveyed various portions of the "Northern Neck."

1752   February 27. Hampshire County, was created at the session of the legislature, effective December 13, 1753, with its seat at Romney. It was named for Hampshire County, England.

1772   February 10. Berkeley County, with Martins-
            burg as its seat, was established at the
            session of the legislature. It was named
            for Norbone Berkeley, Lord Botetourt, member
            of Parliament, governor of Virginia who
            favored the colonial cause.

1774   October. Lord Dunmore, the governor of
            Virginia, leading troops over the mountains
            and a body of militia under General Andrew
            Lewis defeated the Shawnee Indians under
            Cornstalk a crushing blow at Point Pleasant
            where the Ohio and Kanawha Rivers merge.
            Indian attacks on settlers continued until
            after the War of Independence.

1776   October 7. Monongalia County, with its seat
            at Morganton, and Ohio County, with Wheeling
            as its seat, were created.

            The residents of Western Virginia sent in a
            petition requesting that the Continental
            Congress establish a separate government
            for their region.

1777   October 20. Greenbriar County, with its
            seat at Lewisburg, was created, effective
            March 1, 1778.

1784   May 13. Harrison County, with Clarksburg as
            its seat, was established, effective July 20,
            1784.

            It was named for Benjamin Harrison, member
            of the Continental Congress, signer of the
            Declaration of Independence, fifth governor
            of Virginia, father of William Henry Harrison,
            9th President of the United States, and
            great grandfather of Benjamin Harrison, 23rd
            President of the United States.

1785   October 17. Hardy County, with Moorefield
            as its seat, was created at the session of
            the assembly. It was named for Samuel Hardy,
            member of the Virginia house of delegates and
            member of the Continental Congress from Vir-

ginia.

1786   October 16. Randolph County, with its seat
            at Elkins, was established at the session of
            the legislature, effective May 5, 1787. It
            was named for Edmund Jennings Randolph,
            governor of Virginia, member of the Contin-
            ental Congress, delegate from Virginia to
            the United States Constitutional Convention,
            United States Attorney General and Secretary
            of State in the Administration of President
            George Washington.

1787   December 4. Pendleton County, with Franklin
            as its seat, was created, effective May 1,
            1788. It was named for Edmund Pendleton,
            member of the Virginia House of Burgesses
            and house of delegates, member of the Con-
            tinental Congress and delegate to the Vir-
            ginia Constitution Convention of 1788.

1788   November 14. Kanawha County, with Charleston
            as its seat, was established. It was named
            for the Kanawha Indian Tribe.

1790   Population: 55,873.

            The first paper in West Virginia, the
            Potomak Guardian and Berkeley Advertiser,
            was published at Shepherdstown.

1796   November 30. Brooke County was created,
            with its seat at Wellsburg. It was named
            for Robert Brooke, who fought in the Revolu-
            tionary War, was governor of and attorney
            general of Virginia.

1798   December 21. Wood County, with Parkersburg
            as its seat, was established. It was named
            for James Wood, member of the Virginia house
            of burgesses and governor of Virginia.

1799   January 14. Monroe County, with its seat
            at Union, was created. It was named for
            James Monroe, member of the Continental
            Congress, governor of Virginia, United States

Senator from Virginia, later United States
Secretary of State in the Cabinet of President James Madison, and fifth President
of the United States.

1800   Population: 78,592.

1801   January 8. Jefferson County was established,
            with Charles Towne as its seat. It was named
            for Thomas Jefferson, member of the Contin-
            ental Congress, author and signer of the De-
            claration of Independence, United States
            Secretary of State in the administration of
            President George Washington, Vice President
            of the United States under President John
            Adams, and third President of the United
            States.

1804   January 2. Mason County, with Point
            Pleasant as its seat, was created. It was
            named for George Mason, member of the Vir-
            ginia house of burgesses, author of the
            Virginia Declaration of Rights, member of
            Virginia Assembly, and delegate to the
            United States Constitutional Convention.

1809   January 2. Cabell County was established,
            with its seat at Huntington. It was named
            for William H. Cabell, member of the Vir-
            ginia assembly, governor of Virginia, judge
            of the circuit court of appeals and judge
            of the court of appeals.

1810   Population: 105,469.

1814   December 6. Tyler County, with Middlebourne
            as its seat, was created. It was named for
            John Tyler, governor of Virginia, father of
            John Tyler, 10th President of the United
            States, and judge of the Virginia general
            court.

1815   Gas was discovered near Charleston.

1816   December 18. Lewis County, with its seat
            at Weston, was established. It was named
            for Charles Lewis, who served in the Revolu-

tionary War and was killed at the Battle of
Point Pleasant, October 10, 1774.

1818   January 19. Preston County, with Kingwood
              as its seat, was created. It was named for
              James Patten Preston, who fought in the War
              of 1812 and was governor of Virginia.

              January 30. Nicholas County, with its seat
              at Summersville, was established. It was
              named for Wilson Cary Nicholas, United States
              Senator from and governor of Virginia.

1820   Population: 136,808.

1821   December 21. Pocahantas County, with Mar-
              linten as its seat, was created. It was
              named for Pocahantas, daughter of the Indian
              Chief Powhatan who married James Rolfe, a
              colonist and interceded with her father to
              save Captain John Smith.

1824   January 21. Logan County, with its seat at
              Logan, was established. It was named for
              John Logan, who educated a Cayuga Indian
              Chief.

1830   Population: 176,924.

1831   March 1. Jackson County, with Ripley as its
              seat, was created. It was named for Andrew
              Jackson, major general of the United States
              Army, victor of New Orleans, and 7th Presi-
              dent of the United States.

              August. Nat Turner led a black insurrection
              which resulted in the killing of 55 white peo-
              ple in Virginia and possibly 100 blacks.
              20 Blacks were executed for their part in
              the uprising.

1835   March 12. Marshall County, with its seat at
              Moundsville, was established. It was named
              for John Marshall, United States Secretary
              of State in the Cabinet of President John
              Adams and Chief Justice of the United States

Supreme Court.

The first railroad reached Harpers Ferry.

1836   January 15. Braxton County with Sutton as
        its seat, was created. It was named for
        Carter Braxton, member of the Virginia
        house of Burgesses, delegate to the Contin-
        ental Congress, signer of the Declaration
        of Independence and member of the Virginia
        Council of state.

1837   March 17. Mercer County, with Princeton as
        as its seat, was established. It was named
        for Hugh Mercer, physician, brigadier gen-
        eral of the Continental Army who was mor-
        tally wounded at the Battle of Princeton on
        January 3, 1777 and died January 12.

        Marshall University at Huntington and West
        Liberty State College at West Liberty were
        founded.

1840   Population: 224,537.

        March 2. Bethary College received its char-
        ter. It awarded its first degrees in 1844.

1842   January 14. Marion County, with Fairmont as
        its seat, was created. It was named for
        Francis Marion, brigadier general in the
        Continental Army during the Revolutionary
        War, who won the Battle of Eutaw Springs
        and a member of the South Carolina Senate.

        January 18. Wayne County, with its seat at
        Wayne, was established. It was named for
        Anthony Wayne, major general of the Con-
        tinental Army during the Revolutionary War
        and general-in-chief of the Army who de-
        feated the Indians at the Battle of Fallen
        Timber in 1793.

        February 18. Ritchie County was created,
        with Harrisville as its seat. It was named
        for Thomas Ritchie, editor of the Richmond,
        Virginia _Examiner_ and manager of the

Washington, D. C. <u>Union</u>.

March 3. Barbour County, with its seat at Philippi, was established. It was named for Philip Pendleton Barbour, Virginia house of delegates, United States Representative from Virginia to the House of Representatives and Speaker of the House and Associate Justice of the United States Supreme Court.

1844   January 19. Taylor County, with Grafton as its seat, was created. It was named for John Taylor, major and colonel of the army during the Revolutionary War, member of the Virginia house of delegates, and United States Senator from Virginia.

February 4. Doddridge County was established, with West Union as its seat. It was named for Philip Doddridge, member of the Virginia house of delegates and United States Representative from Virginia.

1846   January 10. Wetzel County, with its seat at New Martinsville, was created. Lewis Wetzel an Indian fighter and scout.

1847   March 11. Boone County was established, with Madison as its seat. It was named for Daniel Boone, an explorer and Indian fighter who aided the colonists in the Revolutionary War.

1848   January 15. Hancock County, with New Cumberland as its seat, was created. It was named for John Hancock, first governor of Massachusetts and first signer of the Declaration of Independence.

January 16. Wirt County was established, with Elizabeth as its seat. It was was named for William Wirt, who prosecuted the case against Aaron Burr and was United States Attorney General in the Administration of President James Monroe.

March 11. Putnam County, with its seat at
Winfield, was created. It was named for
Israel Putnam, who served in the French and
Indian and Pontiac's Wars and was a major
general in the Continental Army during the
Revolutionary War.

1850   Population: 302,313.

January 23. Raleigh County, with Beckley as
its seat, was established. It was named for
Sir Walter Raleigh, first Lord Proprietor of
Virginia and servant to Queen Elizabeth.

January 26. Wyoming County, with its seat
at Pineville, was created. It was named for
the Wyoming Indian Tribe.

1851   March 26. Upshur County was established,
with Buckhannon as its seat. It was named
for Abel Parker Upshur, United States Secretary of the Navy and United States Secretary
of State in the Administration of President
John Tyler.

March 29. Pleasants County, with St. Marys
as its seat, was created. It was named for
James Pleasants, member of the Virginia house
of delegates, United States Representative
and Senator from Virginia, and governor of
Virginia.

1856   March 5. Calhoun County, with its seat at
Grantsville, was established. It was named
for John Caldwell Calhoun, United States
Secretary of War in the Administration of
President James Monroe, Vice President of
the United States under Presidents John
Quincy Adams and Andrew Jackson, United
States Senator from South Carolina, and
United States Secretary of State in the
Cabinet of President John Tyler.

March 11. Roane County, with Spencer as its
seat, was created. It was named for Spencer
Roane, justice of the Virginia Supreme Court
of Appeals.

May 7. Tucker County was established, with
its seat at Parsons. It was named for Henry
St. George Tucker, United States Representative from Virginia and Chancellor of the 4th
judicial district of Virginia.

1858   February 20. McDowell County, with Welch as
its seat, was created. It was named for James
McDowell, governor of Virginia and United
States Representative from Virginia.

March 29. Clay County, with its seat at Clay,
was established. It was named for Henry Clay,
United States Representative and Senator from
Kentucky and United States Secretary of State
in the Cabinet of President John Quincy Adams.

1859   October 16. John Brown seized the arsenal at
Harpers Ferry as part of a plan to create an
abolitionist republic in the Appalachian region and fight slavery by using fugitive
blacks and abolitionist whites. Brown was
captured, tried, convicted and eventually
hung at Charleston, Virginia on December 2.

1860   Population: 376,688.

January 10. Webster County, with Webster
Springs as its seat, was created. It was
named for Daniel Webster, United States Re-
presentative from New Hampshire, United
States Representative from Massachusetts,
United States Secretary of State in the Ad-
ministrations of Presidents John Tyler and
Millard Fillmore.

Oil was discovered at Burning Springs.

1861   April 17. Western delegates at the Virginia
secessionist convention indicated their opposition to secession.

April 22. West Virginia Unionists met at
Clarksburg where they began the moverment
which led to the separation of the region
from Virginia. They issued a call for a
convention at Wheeling to meet from May 13-15.

April 29. Colonel Stonewall Jackson assumed
command of the troops at Harpers Ferry.

May 13-15. Western Virginia unionists met
at Wheeling where they initiated the process
of separation from Virginia. The more
cautious members of the convention indicated
that no action should be taken while Virginia
was still in the Union because this would be
a revolutionary step.

May 23. The Virginia ordinance for secession
was ratified by a large majority in the state.
However, 40,000 out of 44,000 voting in the
western counties indicated their opposition.

June 11. A second convention met at Wheeling.
The delegates declared that since the Secession Convention had been called without the
consent of the people, all acts were void,
and that all who adhered to the acts of the
convention had in effect vacated their posts.

June 20. An act for the reorganization of
the government was passed.

June 20. The Wheeling convention created a
loyal Virginia government, with Francis H.
Pierpont as governor.

July 1. A legislature, which was composed
of members from the western counties, who
had been elected on May 23 and some hold-
over senators who had been elected in 1854,
met in Wheeling.

Summer. General McClellan's Union troops
gained control of the larger part of what
was to become West Virginia.

August. Robert E. Lee brought his Confederate troops to Western Virginia in order to
try to regain the losses suffered earlier to
the Union forces. However, the Confederate
troops were defeated.

August 6. The Wheeling Convention reassem-
bled, adopting an ordinance on August 20
which provided for an election to form a
new state and for delegates to a constitutional convention if the vote were favorable.

October 24. An election was held with 18,489
votes cast in favor of establishment of a
new State and only 781 votes against it.

November 26. The constitutional convention
met. It completed the constitution for the
new state on February 18, 1862.

1862   April 11. The state constitution was ratified by the voters: 18,162 for and only 514
against.

May 13. The legislature of the "reorganized"
government agreed to the formation of the
new state.

June 20. Arthur I. Boreman, Unionist Republican, became governor of West Virginia
and served in the post until his resignation
on February 26, 1869.

September 15. General "Stonewall" Jackson
captured Harpers Ferry.

December 31. President Abraham Lincoln gave
his approval to the Enabling Act which admitted West Virginia to the Union on condition that a provision providing for the
gradual abolition of slavery was inserted
in the Constitution.

1863   February 12. The Constitutional Convention
met and agreed to insert the provision for
gradual abolition in slavery in the constitution.

March 26. The citizens ratified the revised
constitution.

April 20. President Abraham Lincoln issued

a proclamation admitting West Virginia to
the Union after a 60-day period on June 20.

June 20. West Virginia became the 35th
state of the Union.

November. Union troops launched an attack
against Lewisburg.

1865   February 3. The state legislature ratified
            the 13th Amendment to the United States Con-

1866   February 1. Mineral County, with Keyser as
            its seat, was created.

            February 14. Grant County, with its seat at
            Petersburg, was established. It was named
            for Ulysses S. Grant, major general of the
            United States Army during the Civil War, who
            received Robert E. Lee's surrender at Ap-
            pomattox Court House on April 9, 1865, and
            later 18th President of the United States.

            March 10. The United States Congress passed
            a joing resolution recognizing the transfer
            of Berkeley and Jefferson Counties from Vir-
            ginia to West Virginia.

1867   February 23. Lincoln County was created,
            with its seat at Hamlin. It was named for
            Abraham Lincoln, United States Representa-
            tive from Illinois and 10th President of the
            United States.

            West Virginia University at Morgantown was
            founded as the Agricultural College of West
            Virginia. Its first classes were held in
            1868 as well as its present name adopted.
            Fairmont State College was also established.

1869   February 27. Daniel D. T. Farnsworth, pre-
            sident of the state senate, a Republican,
            became governor of the state upon the resig-
            nation of Governor Arthur I. Boreman.
            Farnsworth served in the office until March 3,
            1869.

March 4. William E. Stevenson, Republican, became governor of West Virginia. He served in the office until March 3, 1871.

The state legislature ratified the 15th Amendment to the United States Constitution.

1870   Population: 442,014.

1871   February 27. Summers County, with Hinton as its seat, was established. It was named for George William Summers, member of the Virginia house of delegates and United States Representative from Virginia.

March 4. John Jeremiah Jacob, Democrat and Independent, became governor of the state. He remained in the office until March 3, 1877.

The United States Supreme Court decided in favor of West Virginia regarding the transfer of Berkeley and Jefferson Counties.

Alderson-Braddus College at Philippi and Shepherd College at Shepherdstown were founded.

1872   August 22. A new state constitution was adopted by the citizens.

Concord College at Athens and Glenville State College at Glenville were established.

1873   The Chesapeake and Ohio Railroad was completed in the State.

1877   March 4. Henry Mason Mathews, Democrat, became governor of West Virginia. He served in the office until March 3, 1881.

1880   Population: 618,457.

1881   January 16. Nathan Goff, Jr., became Secretary of the Navy in the Cabinet of President Rutherford B. Hayes.

March 4.   Jacob B. Jackson, Democrat, became governor of the state. He served in
the office until March 3, 1885.

1885   March 4.   Emanuel Willis Wilson, Democrat,
who had been elected in 1884, became governor of West Virginia. He continued to serve
in the office for almost one year beyond
the expiration of his term because of a
dispute over the 1888 election. He remained
in the post until February 5, 1890.

1888   The following academic institutions of higher
learning were organized: Morris Harvey College at Charleston and Salem College.

1890   February 6.   Aretas Brooks Fleming, Democrat, who had been elected in 1888 and whose
election was disputed for over a year, became governor of the state. He served in
the office until March 4, 1893.

West Virginia Wesleyan College was founded
at Buckhannon.

1891   December 2.   Stephen B. Elkins was appointed
United States Secretary of War by President
Benjamin Harrison. He assumed his office
as a member of the cabinet on December 24.

West Virginia State College was founded.

1893   March 4.   William A. McCorckle, Democrat,
who had been elected in 1892, became governor of the state. He served in the office
until March 3, 1897.

1895   January 30.   Mingo County, with Williamson
as its seat, was established. It was named
for the Mingo Indian Tribe.

March 1.   William L. Wilson was appointed
Postmaster General of the United States by
President Grover Cleveland. Wilson assumed
his office as a member of the Cabinet on
April 4, 1895.

Bluefield State College at Bluefield and
West Virginia Institute of Technology at
Montgomery were founded.

1897   March 4. George W. Atkinson, Republican,
              who had been elected in 1896, became gover-
              nor of the state. He served in the office
              until March 4, 1901.

              July 2. Coalminers went out on strike in
              West Virginia, Pennsylvania and Ohio. The
              strike ended September 11 with the miners
              winning an eight-hour work day, semi-month-
              ly pay, the end of company stores and
              biennial conferences.

1900   Population: 958,000.

1901   March 4. Albert B. White, Republican, who
              had been elected in 1900, became governor
              of West Virginia. He served in the office
              until March 4, 1905.

1904   Davis and Elkins College was Founded at
              Elkins.

1905   March 4. William M. O. Dawson, Republican,
              who had been elected in 1904, became gover-
              nor of the state. He served in the office
              until March 4, 1909.

1909   March 4. William E. Glasscock, Republican,
              who had been elected in 1908, became gover-
              nor of West Virginia. He served in the
              office until March 4, 1913.

1910   Population: 1,221,119.

1912   Paint Creek Miners went out on strike in
              order to gain recognition of the United
              Mine Workers of America and the signing of
              a union contract.

1913   January 31. The state legislature ratified
              the 16th Amendment to the United States
              Constitution.

February 4. The state legislature ratified
the 17th Amendment to the United States
Constitution.

March 4. Henry D. Hatfield, Republican, who
had been elected in 1912, became governor
of the state. He served in the office until
March 4, 1917.

March. Governor Henry D. Hatfield visited
the Point Creek Mine region in order to try
to help settle the strike. He treated many
miners and their families in his capacity as
as physician.

1915   The United States Supreme Court ruled that
            West Virginia owed Virginia $12,393,929.50
            as part of the state debt at the time of its
            separation. The debt was finally paid off
            in 1939.

1917   March 4. John T. Cornwell, Democrat, who
            had been elected in 1916, became governor
            of the state. He served in the office until
            March 4, 1921.

1919   January 9. The state legislature ratified
            the 18th Amendment to the United States Con-
            stitution.

1920   Population: 1,463,701.

            March 10. The state legislature ratified
            the 19th Amendment to the United States
            Constitution.

1921   March 4. Ephraim F. Morgan, Republican, who
            had been elected in 1920, became governor of
            West Virginia. He served in the position
            until March 4, 1925.

            Battles occurred between miners and owners
            in Logan County.

1924   April 1. A strike began against the north-
            ern coal operators. A bitter struggle went

on for three years.

November 21. Howard M. Gore was appointed
Secretary of Agriculture by President Calvin Coolidge. Gore assumed his office as
a member of the Cabinet.

1925   March 4. Howard M. Gore, Republican, who
            had been elected in 1924, became governor
            of the state. He served in the office
            until March 4, 1929.

1929   March 4. William G. Conley, Republican,
            who had been elected in 1928, became gover-
            nor of the state. He served in the post
            until March 4, 1933.

1930   Population: 1,729,205.

1932   July 30. The state legislature ratified
            the 20th Amendment to the United States Con-
            stitution.

            The first radio station in the state began
            broadcasting from Huntington, WSAZ.

1933   March 4. Herman G. Kump, Democrat, who had
            been elected in 1932, became governor of
            West Virginia. He remained in the post
            until January 18, 1937.

            July 25. The state legislature ratified
            the 21st Amendment to the United States
            Constitution.

1937   January 18. Homer A. Holt, Democrat, who
            had been elected in 1936, became governor
            of the state. He served in the office until
            January 13, 1941.

1939   West Virginia made the final payment of its
            debt to Virginia.

1940   Population: 1,901,974.

1941   January 13. Matthew M. Neely, Democrat, who

had been elected in 1940, became governor
of West Virginia. He served in the post
until January 15, 1945.

1943   Geologists found large salt deposits in the
            northwestern counties.

1945   January 15. Clarence W. Meadows, Democrat,
            who had been elected in 1944, became gover-
            nor of the state. He served in the post
            until January 17, 1949.

1946   Several major chemical industries began
            operating in the Ohio River Valley.

1949   January 17. Okey L. Patteson, Democrat, who
            had been elected in 1948, became governor
            of West Virginia, remaining in the post
            until January 19, 1953.

            March 23. Louis A. Johnson was appointed
            United States Secretary of Defense by Pre-
            sident Harry S. Truman. Johnson assumed
            his office as a member of the Cabinet on
            March 28.

            The first television station in the state,
            WSAZ-TV, began broadcasting from Huntington.

1950   Population: 2,005,552.

1953   January 19. William C. Marland, Democrat,
            who had been elected in 1952, became gover-
            nor in the state. He served in the office
            until January 14, 1957.

1954   Wheeling College was established at Wheeling.

1956   November 6. Residents of the state ap-
            proved a bond which provided a bonus for
            Korean War Veterans.

1957   January 14. Cecil H. Underwood, Republican,
            who had been elected in 1956, became gover-
            nor of the state. He served in the office
            until January 16, 1961.

1959   The National Radio Astronomy Observatory be-
            gan operating at Green Bank.

1960   Population: 1,860,421.

1961   January 16. William W. Barron, Democrat,
            who had been elected in 1960, became gover-
            nor of West Virginia. He served in the
            office until January 18, 1965.

            February 9. The state legislature ratified
            the 23rd Amendment to the United States
            Constitution.

1962   The state legislature approved the use of
            funds to supply birth control information
            and aid to people on welfare.

1965   January 18. The state legislature abolished
            capital punishment.

                    Julett C. Smith, Democrat, who
            had been elected in 1964, became governor of
            West Virginia. He remained in the post until
            January 3, 1969.

            March. The United States Congress passed the
            Appalachian Regional Redevelopment Act which
            provided federal aid for revitalizing the
            economy.

1966   January 20. The state legislature ratified
            the 25th Amendment to the United States Con-
            stitution.

            The state legislature passed a minimum wage
            law.

1968   Several explosions and a fire wrecked a
            coal mine, taking 78 lives. This serious
            disaster led to the enactment of new mine
            safety legislation.

1969   January 3. Arch A. Moore, Democrat, who had
            been elected in 1968, became governor of
            West Virginia. He was reelected in 1972 and

served until January, 1977.

1970   Population: 1,744,237.

West Virginia College of Graduate Studies
was established.

1971   March 13. Congressional redistricting was
enacted. West Virginia lost one seat as
a result of the 1970 census.

April 28. The state legislature ratified
the 26th Amendment to the United States Constitution.

1972   February 26. A coalwaste dam at Buffalo
Creek collapsed, causing a flood and killing
118 people.

May 31. The Environmental Protection Agency
approved the state's clean air proposals.

The state legislature ratified the Equal
Rights Amendment to the United States Constitution.

August 11. A miners strike, unauthorized
by the United Mine Workers of America began.

1975   December 18. Governor Arch A. Moore was
indicted by a federal grand jury in Charleston on a charge of extorting $25,000 from a
businessman who was trying to obtain a state
bank charter.

1976   July 16. A wild cat miners strike began.
It ended August 16.

November 2. John Davison Rockefeller IV,
Democrat, was elected governor of the state.

1977   January. John Davison Rockefeller IV was
inaugurated as governor of West Virginia.

March 17. President Jimmy Carter partici-
pated in a seminar on energy.

BIOGRAPHICAL DIRECTORY

The selected list of governors, United States
Senators and Members of the House of Representatives
for West Virginia, 1863-1977, includes all persons
listed in the Chronology for whom basic biographical
data was readily available. Older biographical
sources are frequently in conflict on certain individuals, and in such cases the source most commonly
cited by later authorities was preferred.

ALDERSON, John Duffy
    Democrat
    b. Nicholas Court House (now Summersville),
        W. Va., November 29, 1834
    d. Richwood, W. Va., December 5, 1910
    U. S. Representative, 1889-95

ALLEN, Robert Edward Lee
    Democrat
    b. Lima W. Va., November 28, 1865
    d. Mountain Lake Park, Md., January 28,
        1851
    U. S. Representative, 1923-25

ATKINSON, George Wesley
    Republican
    b. Charleston, Va. (now W. Va.), June
        29, 1845
    d. April 4, 1925
    U. S. Representative, 1897-1901

AVIS, Samuel Brashear
    Republican
    b. Harrisonburg, Va., February 19, 1872
    d. Charleston, W. Va., June 8, 1924
    U. S. Representative, 1913-15

BACHMANN, Carl George
    Republican
    b. Wheeling, W. Va., May 14, 1890
    U. S. Representative, 1925-33; Minority
        Whip, 72nd Congress, 1931-33

BAILEY, Cleveland Monroe
    Democrat
    b. on a farm near St. Mary's, W. Va., July
        15, 1886
    d. Charleston, W. Va., July 13, 1865
    U. S. Representative, 1945-47, 1949-63

BARRON, William Wallace
    Democrat
    b. Elkins, W. Va., December 8, 1911
    Governor of West Virginia, 1961-65

BLAIR, Jacob Beeson
    Unionist (Virginia/West Virginia)
    b. Parkersburg, Va. (now W. Va.), April
      11, 1821
    d. Salt Lake City, Utah, February 12,
      1901
    U. S. Representative, 1861-63 (Virginia),
      1863-65 (West Virginia)

BOREMAN, Arthur Inghram
    Republican
    b. Waynesburg, Pa., July 24, 1823
    d. Parkersburg, W. Va., April 19, 1896
    Governor of West Virginia, 1863-69
    U. S. Senator, 1869-75

BOWERS, George Meade
    Republican
    b. Gerrardstown, W. Va., September 13,
      1863
    d. Martinsburg, W. Va., December 7, 1925
    U. S. Representative, 1916-23

BOWMAN, Frank Llewellyn
    Republican
    b. Masontown, Pa., January 21, 1879
    d. Washington, D. C., September 15, 1936
    U. S. Representative, 1925-33

BROWN, William Gay
    Unionist (Virginia/West Virginia)
    b. Kingwood, Va. (now W. Va.), September
      25, 1800
    d. Kingwood, W. Va., April 19, 1884
    U. S. Representative, 1845-49 (Democrat -
      Virginia), 1861-63 (Unionist - Vir-
      ginia), 1863-65 (Unionist - West
      Virginia)

BROWN, William Gay, Jr.
    Democrat
    b. Lingwood, Va. (now W. Va.), April 7,
      1856
    d. Washington, D. C., March 9, 1916
    U. S. Representative, 1911-16

BURNSIDE, Maurice Gwinn
    Democrat
    b. near Columbia, S. C., August 23, 1902
    U. S. Representative, 1949-53, 1955-57

BYRD, Richard Carlyle
    Democrat
    b. North Wilkesboro, N. C., January 15,
        1918
    U. S. Representative, 1953-59
    U. S. Senator, 1959-

CAMDEN, Johnson Newlon
    Democrat
    b. Collins Settlement, Va. (now W. Va.),
        March 6, 1828
    d. Baltimore, Md., April 25, 1908
    U. S. Senator, 1881-87, 1893-95

CAPERTON, Allen Taylor
    Democrat
    b. near Union, Va. (now W. Va.), November
        21, 1810
    d. Washington, D. C., July 26, 1876
    U. S. Senator, 1875-76

CHILTON, William Edwin
    Democrat
    b. Colesmouth (now St. Albans), Va. (now
        W. Va.), March 17, 1858
    d. Charleston, W. Va., November 7, 1939
    U. S. Senator, 1911-17

CONLEY, William Gustavus
    Republican
    b. Kingwood, W. Va., January 8, 1866
    d. October 21, 1940
    Governor of West Virginia, 1929-33

COOPER, Edward
    Republican
    b. Treverton, Pa., February 26, 1873
    d. in a hospital in Bluefield, W. Va.,
        March 1, 1928
    U. S. Representative, 1915-19

CORNWELL, John J.
    Democrat
    b. Ritchie County, W. Va., July 11, 1867
    d. September 8, 1953
    Governor of West Virginia, 1917-21

DAVIS, Henry Gassaway
    Democrat
    b. Baltimore, Md., November 16, 1823
    d. Washington, D. C., March 11, 1916
    U. S. Senator, 1871-83

DAVIS, John James
    Democrat
    b. Clarksburg, Va. (now W. Va.), May 5,
        1835
    d. Clarksburg, W. Va., March 19, 1919
    U. S. Representative, 1871-75

DAVIS, John William
    Democrat
    b. Clarksburg, W. Va., April 13, 1873
    d. Charleston, S. C., March 24, 1955
    U. S. Representative, 1905-07

DAWSON, William Mercer Owens
    Republican
    b. Bloomington, Md., May 21, 1853
    d. March 12, 1916
    Governor of West Virginia, 1905-09

DAYTON, Alston Gordon
    Republican
    b. Philippi, Va. (now W. Va.), October 18,
        1857
    d. Battle Creek, Mich., July 30, 1920
    U. S. Representative, 1895-1905

DORR, Charles Philips
    Republican
    b. Miltonsburg, Ohio, August 12, 1852
    d. on his estate "Clover Lick Farms," at
        Cloverlick, near Marlinton, W. Va.,
        October 8, 1914
    U. S. Representative, 1897-99

DOVENER, Blackburn Barrett
    Republican
    b. Tays Valley, Va. (now W. Va.), April
        20, 1842
    d. Glen Echo, Md., May 9, 1914
    U. S. Representative, 1895-1907

DUVAL, Isaac Harding
    Republican
    b. Wellsburg, Va. (now W. Va.), September
        1, 1824
    d. Wellsburg, W. Va., July 10, 1902
    U. S. Representative, 1869-71

ECHOLS, Leonard Sidney
    Republican
    b. Madison, W. Va., October 30, 1871
    d. Charleston, W. Va., May 9, 1946
    U. S. Representative, 1919-23

EDMISTON, Andrew
    Democrat
    b. Weston, W. Va., November 13, 1892
    d. Weston, W. Va., August 28, 1966
    U. S. Representative, 1933-43

ELKINS, Davis
    Republican
    b. Washington, D. C., January 24, 1876
    d. Richmond, Va., January 5, 1959
    U. S. Senator, 1911, 1919-25

ELKINS, Stephen Benton
    Republican (New Mexico/West Virginia)
    b. Perry County, Ohio, September 26, 1841
    d. Washington, D. C., January 4, 1911
    U. S. Representative (Territorial Delegate
      New Mexico), 1873-77
    U. S. Secretary of War, 1891-93
    U. S. Senator (West Virginia), 1895-1911

ELLIS, Hubert Summers
    Republican
    b. Hurricane, W. Va., July 6, 1887
    d. Huntington, W. Va., December 3, 1959
    U. S. Representative, 1943-49

ENGLAND, Edward Theodore
    Republican
    b. Gay, W. Va., September 29, 1869
    d. Cleveland, Ohio, September 9, 1934
    U. S. Representative, 1927-29

FARNSWORTH, Daniel D. T.
    Republican
    Governor of West Virginia, 1869

FAULKNER, Charles James
    Democrat
    b. Martinsburg, Va. (now W. Va.), Septem-
      ber, 21, 1847
    d. on his family estate "Boydville," near
      Martinsburg, W. Va., January 13, 1929
    U. S. Senator, 1887-99

FLEMING, Arestas Brooks
    Democrat
    b. Fairmont, W. Va., October 15, 1838
    d. October 13, 1923
    Governor of West Virginia, 1890-93

FREER, Romeo Hoyt
    Republican

b. Bazetta, Ohio, November 9, 1846
d. Harrisburg, W. Va., May 9, 1913
U. S. Representative, 1899-1901

GAINES, Joseph Holt
Republican
b. Washington, D. C., September 3, 1864
d. Montgomery, W. Va., April 12, 1951
U. S. Representative, 1901-11

GIBSON, Eustace
Democrat
b. Culpepper County, Va., October 4,
    1842
d. Clifton Forge, Va., December 10, 1900
U. S. Representative, 1883-87

GLASSCOCK, William Ellsworth
Republican
b. near Arnettsville, W. Va., December 13,
    1862
d. April 12, 1925
Governor of West Virginia, 1909-13

GOFF, Guy Despard
Republican
b. Clarksburg, W. Va., September 13, 1866
d. at his winter home, Thomasville, Ga.,
    January 7, 1933
U. S. Senator, 1925-31

GOFF, Nathan
Republican
b. Clarksburg, Va. (now W. Va.), February
    8, 1843
d. Clarksburg, W. Va., April 24, 1920
U. S. Secretary of the Navy, 1881
U. S. Representative, 1883-89
U. S. Senator, 1913-19

GOODYKOONTZ, Wells
Republican
b. near Newton, Va., June 3, 1872
d. in a hospital, Cincinnati, Ohio, March
    2, 1944
U. S. Representative, 1919-23

GORE, Howard Mason
Republican
b. Clarksburg, W. Va., October 12, 1887
d. June 20, 1947
U. S. Secretary of Agriculture, 1924-25
Governor of West Virginia, 1925-29

HAGANS, John Marshall
    Republican
    b. Brandonville, Va. (now W. Va.), August
        13, 1838
    d. Morgantown, W. Va., June 17, 1900
    U. S. Representative, 1873-75

HAMILTON, John M.
    Democrat
    b. Weston, Va. (now W. Va.), March 16,
        1855
    d. Grantsville, W. Va., December 27, 1916
    U. S. Representative, 1911-13

HATFIELD, Henry Drury
    Republican
    b. Sidney post office, Logan County, W.
        Va., September 15, 1875
    d. Huntington, W. Va., October 23, 1962
    Governor of West Virginia, 1913-17
    U. S. Senator, 1929-35

HECHLER, Kenneth
    Democrat
    b. Nassau County, near Roslyn, Long Island,
        N. Y., September 20, 1914
    U. S. Representative, 1959-

HEDRICK, Erland Harold
    Democrat
    b. Barn, W. Va., August 9, 1894
    d. Beckley, W. Va., September 20, 1954
    U. S. Representative, 1945-53

HEREFORD, Frank
    Democrat
    b. near Warrenton, Va., July 4, 1825
    d. Union, W. Va., December 21, 1891
    U. S. Representative, 1871-77
    U. S. Senator, 1877-81

HOBLITZELL, John Dempsey, Jr.
    Republican
    b. Parkesburg, W. Va., December 30, 1912
    U. S. Senator, 1958

HOGE, John Blair
    Democrat
    b. Richmond, Va., February 2, 1825
    d. Martinsburg, W. Va., March 1, 1896
    U. S. Representative, 1881-83

HOGG, Charles Edgar
    Democrat
    b. on a farm near Point Pleasant Va.
        (now W. Va.), December 21, 1852
    d. Point Pleasant, W. Va., June 14, 1935
    U. S. Representative, 1887-89

HOGG, Robert Lynn
    Republican
    b. Point Pleasant, W. Va., December 30,
        1893
    U. S. Representative, 1930-33

HOLT, Homer Adams
    Democrat
    b. Lewisburg, W. Va., March 1, 1898
    d. January 16, 1975
    Governor of West Virginia, 1933-37

HOLT, Rush Dew
    Democrat
    b. Weston, W. Va., June 19, 1905
    d. Bethesda, Md., February 8, 1955
    U. S. Senator, 1935-41

HORNOR, Lynn Sedgwick
    Democrat
    b. Clarksburg, W. Va., November 3, 1874
    d. Washington, D. C., September 23, 1933
    U. S. Representative, 1931-33

HUBBARD, Chester Dorman
    Republican
    b. Hamden, Conn., November 25, 1814
    d. Wheeling, W. Va., August 23, 1891
    U. S. Representative, 1865-69

HUBBARD, William Pallister
    Republican
    b. Wheeling, Va. (now W. Va.), December
        24, 1843
    d. Wheeling, W. Va., December 5, 1921
    U. S. Representative, 1907-11

HUGHES, James Anthony
    Republican
    b. near Corunna, Ontario, Canada, Febru-
        ary 27, 1861
    d. Marion, Ohio, March 2, 1930
    U. S. Representative, 1901-05, 1927-30

HULING, James Hall
    Republican

b. Williamsport, Pa., March 24, 1844
d. Charleston, W. Va., April 23, 1918
U. S. Representative, 1895-97

JACKSON, Jacob B.
Democrat
Governor of West Virginia, 1881-85

JACKSON, James Monroe
Democrat
b. Parkersburg, Va. (now W. Va.), De-
    cember 3, 1825
d. Parkersburg, W. Va., February 14, 1901
U. S. Representative, 1889-90

JACOB, John Jeremiah
Democrat/Independent
Governor of West Virginia, 1871-77

Johnson, George William
Democrat
b. near Charles Town, W. Va., November 10,
    1869
d. Martinsburg, W. Va., February 24, 1944
U. S. Representative, 1923-25, 1933-43

KEE, James
Democrat
b. Bluefield, W. Va., April 15, 1917
U. S. Representative, 1965-

KEE, John
Democrat
b. Glenville, W. Va., August 22, 1874
d. Washington, D. C., May 8, 1951
U. S. Representative, 1933-51

KEE, Maude Elizabeth
Democrat
b. Ratford, Va.
U. S. Representative, 1951-65

KENNA, John Edward
Democrat
b. near St. Albans, Va. (now W. VA.),
    April 10, 1848
d. Washington, D. C., January 11, 1893
U. S. Representative, 1877-83
U. S. Senator, 1883-93

KILGORE, Harley Martin
Democrat
b. Brown, W. Va., January 11, 1893

d. Bethesda, Md., February 28, 1956
U. S. Senator, 1941-56

KITCHEN, Bethuel Middleton
Republican
b. Ganotown, Va. (now W. Va.), March
    21, 1812
d. Shanghai, W. Va., December 15, 1895
U. S. Representative, 1867-69

KUMP, Herman Guy
Democrat
b. Capon Springs, W. Va., October 31, 1877
d. February 14, 1962
Governor of West Virginia, 1933-37

LAIRD, William Ramsey III
Democrat
b. Keswick, Calif., June 2, 1916
U. S. Senator, 1956

LATHAM, George Robert
Republican
b. near Haymarket, Va., March 9, 1832
d. Buckhannon, W. Va., December 16, 1917
U. S. Representative, 1865-67

LILLY, Thomas Jefferson
Democrat
b. Dunns, W. Va., June 3, 1878
d. Sweet Springs, W. Va., April 2, 1936
U. S. Representative, 1923-25

LITTLEPAGE, Adam Brown
Democrat
b. near Charleston, Va. (now W. Va.), April
    14, 1859
d. Charleston, W. Va., June 29, 1921
U. S. Representative, 1911-13, 1915-19

LOVE, Francis Johnson
Republican
b. Cadiz, Ohio, January 23, 1901
U. S. Representative, 1947-49

MACCORKLE, William Alexander
Democrat
b. Lexington, Va., May 7, 1857
d. September 24, 1930
Governor of West Virginia, 1893-97

MARLAND, William Casey
Democrat

b. Johnson City, Ill., March 26, 1918
d. November 1965
Governor of West Virginia, 1953-57

MARTIN, Benjamin Franklin
    Democrat
    b. near Farmington, Va. (now W. Va.),
        October 2, 1828
    d. Grafton, W. Va., January 20, 1895
    U. S. Representative, 1877-81

MATHEWS, Henry Mason
    Democrat
    Governor of West Virginia, 1877-81

MCGREW, James Clark
    Republican
    b. near Brandonville, Va. (now W. Va.),
        September 14, 1813
    d. Kingwood, W. Va., September 18, 1910
    U. S. Representative, 1869-73

MEADOWS, Clarence Watson
    Democrat
    b. Beckley, W. Va., February 11, 1904
    d. September 12, 1961
    Governor of West Virginia, 1945-49

MOLLOHAN, Robert Homer
    Democrat
    b. Grantsville, W. Va., September 18, 1909
    U. S. Representative, 1953-57, 1969-

MOORE, Arch Alfred, Jr.
    Republican
    b. Moundsville, W. Va., April 16, 1923
    U. S. Representative, 1957-69
    Governor of West Virginia, 1969-

MORGAN, Ephraim Franklin
    Republican
    b. Marion County, W. Va., January 16, 1869
    d. January 15, 1950
    Governor of West Virginia, 1921-25

MOSS, Hunter Holmes, Jr.
    Republican
    b. Parkersburg, W. Va., May 26, 1874
    d. Atlantic City, N. J., July 15, 1916
    U. S. Representative, 1913-16

NEAL, William Elmer
    Republican

b. on a farm near Proctorville, Ohio,
     October 14, 1875
d. Huntington, W. Va., November 12, 1959
U. S. Representative, 1953-55, 1957-59

NEELY, Matthew Mansfield
Democrat
b. Grove, W. Va., November 9, 1874
d. at the Naval Hospital, Bethesda, Md.,
     January 18, 1958
U. S. Representative, 1913-21
U. S. Senator, 1923-29, 1931-41
Governor of West Virginia, 1941-45
U. S. Representative, 1945-47
U. S. Senator, 1949-58

O'BRIEN, William Smith
Democrat
b. Audra, near Philippi, Va. (now W. Va.),
     January 8, 1862
d. Buckhannon, W. Va., August 10, 1948
U. S. Representative, 1927-29

PATTESON, Okey Leonidas
Democrat
b. Dinges, W. Va., September 14, 1898
Governor of West Virginia, 1949-53

PENDLETON, John Overton
Democrat
b. Wellsburg, Va. (now W. Va.), July 4,
     1851
d. Wheeling, W. Va., December 24, 1916
U. S. Representative, 1889-90, 1891-95

POLSLEY, Daniel Haymond
Republican
b. Palatine, Va. (now W. Va.), November
     28, 1803
d. Point Pleasant, W. Va., October 14, 1877
U. S. Representative, 1867-69

PRICE, Samuel
----
b. Fauquier County, Va., July 28, 1805
d. Lewisburg, W. Va., February 25, 1884
U. S. Senator, 1876-77

RAMSEY, Robert Lincoln
Democrat
b. Durham, England, March 24, 1877
d. Wheeling, W. Va., November 14, 1956
U. S. Representative, 1933-39, 1941-43

1949-53

RANDOLPH, Jennings
Democrat
b. Salem, W. Va., March 8, 1902
U. S. Representative, 1933-47
U. S. Senator, 1958-

REED, Stuart Felix
Republican
b. near Philippi, W. Va., January 8, 1866
d. Washington, D. C., July 4, 1935
U. S. Representative, 1917-25

REVERCOMB, William Chapman
Republican
b. Covington, Va., July 20, 1895
U. S. Senator, 1942-49, 1956-59

ROCKEFELLER, John Davison IV
Democrat
b. June 18, 1937
Governor of West Virginia, 1977-

ROHRBOUGH, Edward Gay
Republican
b. near Buckhannon, W. Va., 1874
d. Washington, D. C., December 12, 1956
U. S. Representative, 1943-45, 1947-49

ROSENBLOOM, Benjamin Louis
Republican
b. Braddock, Pa., June 3, 1880
d. Cleveland Clinic, Cleveland, Ohio,
    March 22, 1965
U. S. Representative, 1921-25

ROSIER, Joseph
Democrat
b. Williamsburg, W. Va., January 24, 1870
d. Fairmont, W. Va., October 7, 1951
U. S. Senator, 1941-42

SCHIFFLER, Andrew Charles
Republican
b. Wheeling, W. Va., August 10, 1889
d. Wheeling, W. Va., March 27, 1970
U. S. Representative, 1939-41, 1943-45

SCOTT, Nathan Bay
Republican
b. near Quaker City, Ohio, December 18,
    1842

d. Washington, D. C., January 2, 1924
U. S. Senator, 1899-1911

SHOTT, Hugh Ike
Republican
b. Staunton, Va., September 3, 1866
d. Bluefield, W. Va., October 12, 1953
U. S. Representative, 1929-33
U. S. Senator, 1942-43

SLACK, John Mark, Jr.
Democrat
b. Charleston, W. Va., March 18, 1915
U. S. Representative, 1959-

SMITH, Charles Brooks
Republican
b. Elizabeth, Va., February 24, 1844
d. Parkersburg, W. Va., December 7, 1899
U. S. Representative, 1890-91

SMITH, Hulett Carlson
Republican
b. Beckley, W. Va., October 21, 1918
Governor of West Virginia, 1965-69

SMITH, Joseph Luther
Democrat
b. Marshes (now Glen Daniel), W. Va.,
   May 22, 1880
d. Beckley, W. Va., August 23, 1962
U. S. Representative, 1929-45

SNYDER, Charles Philip
Democrat
b. Charleston, Va. (now W. Va.), June 9,
   1847
d. Vineland, N. J., August 21, 1915
U. S. Representative, 1883-89

SNYDER, Melvin Claude
Republican
b. Albright, W. Va., October 29, 1898
U. S. Representative, 1947-49

STAGGERS, Hanley Orrin
Democrat
b. Keyser, W. Va., August 3, 1907
U. S. Representative, 1949-

STEVENSON, William E.
Republican
Governor of West Virginia, 1869-71

STROTHER, James French
Republican
b. near Pearisburg, Va., June 29, 1868
d. April 10, 1930
U. S. Representative, 1925-29

STURGISS, George Cookman
Republican
b. Poland, Ohio, August 16, 1842
d. Morgantown, W. Va., February 26, 1925
U. S. Representative, 1907-11

SUTHERLAND, Howard
Republican
b. near Kirkwood, Mo., September 8, 1865
d. Washington, D. C., March 12, 1950
U. S. Representative, 1913-17
U. S. Senator, 1917-23

TAYLOR, James Alfred
Democrat
b. Ironton, Ohio, September 25, 1878
d. Montgomery, W. Va., June 9, 1956
U. S. Representative, 1923-27

UNDERWOOD, Cecil H.
Republican
b. Josephs Mills, W. Va., November 5, 1922
Governor of West Virginia, 1957-61

VAN WINKLE, Peter Godwin
Unionist
b. New York, N. Y., September 7, 1808
d. Parkersburg, W. Va., April 15, 1872
U. S. Senator, 1863-69

WATSON, Clarence Wayland
Democrat
b. Fairmont, W. Va., May 8, 1864
d. Cincinnati, Ohio, May 24, 1940
U. S. Senator, 1911-13

WHALEY, Kellian Van Rensalear
Republican (Virginia/West Virginia)
b. Onondaga County, near Utica, N. Y.,
    May 6, 1821
d. Point Pleasant, W. Va., May 20, 1876
U. S. Representative, 1861-63 (Virginia),
    1863-67 (West Virginia)

WHITE, Albert Blakeslee
Republican

b. Cleveland, Ohio, September 22, 1856
d. ----
Governor of West Virginia, 1901-05

WILLEY, Waitman Thomas
---- (Virginia/West Virginia)
b. Monongalia County, Va. (in what is now
    part of Marion County, W. Va.), October
    18, 1811
d. Morgantown, W. Va., May 2, 1900
U. S. Senator, 1861-63 (Virginia),
    1863-71 (West Virginia)

WILSON, Benjamin
Democrat
b. Wilsonburg, Va. (now W. Va.), April 30,
    1825
d. Clarksburg, W. Va., April 26, 1901
U. S. Representative, 1875-83

WILSON, Emanuel Willis
Democrat
Governor of West Virginia, 1885-90

WILSON, William Lyne
Democrat
b. near Charles Town, Va. (now W. Va.),
    May 3, 1843
d. Lexington, Va., October 17, 1900
U. S. Representative, 1883-95
U. S. Postmaster General, 1895-97

WITCHER, John Seashoal
Republican
b. Cabell County, Va. (now W. Va.),
    July 15, 1839
d. Salt Lake City, Utah, July 8, 1906
U. S. Representative, 1869-71

WOLVERTON, John Marshall
Republican
b. Big Bend, W. Va., January 31, 1872
d. Richwood, W. Va., August 19, 1944
U. S. Representative, 1925-27, 1929-31

WOODYARD, Harry Chapman
Republican
b. Spencer, W. Va., November 13, 1867
d. Spencer, W. Va., June 21, 1929
U. S. Representative, 1903-11, 1916-23,
    1925-27

PROMINENT PERSONALITIES

The following select list of prominent persons of West Virginia has been selected to indicate the valuable contributions they have made to American life.

BAKER, Newton D.
    b. Martinsburg, W. Va., December 3, 1871
    d. December 25, 1937
    City Solicitor, Cleveland, 1902-12
    Mayor of Cleveland, 1912-16
    U. S. Secretary of War, 1916-21
    Member, Permanent Court of Arbitration at
        The Hague, 1928

BENT, Charles
    b. Charles Town, Va. (now W. Va.), November
        11, 1799
    d. Taos, N. Mex., January 19, 1847
    Founded fur trading company: Bent and St.
        Vrain, 1828
    Constructed Bent's Fort near present day
        La Junta, 1828-32
    Led trading caravans to Santa Fe, 1829, 1832,
        1833
    Civil governor of New Mexico after U. S.
        conquest, 1846-47
    Killed in Mexican and Indian revolt, Taos, N. Mex.

BUCK, Pearl
    b. Hillsboro, W. Va., 1892
    Author: The Good Earth, 1931 (Awarded Pulitzer
        Prize, 1932)
            A House Divided, 1935
            Fighting Angel, 1936
            Dragon Seed, 1942
    Awarded Nobel Prize in Literature, 1938

COOKE, Philip Pendleton
    b. Martinsburg, Va. (now W. Va.), October
        26, 1816
    d. January 20, 1850
    Lawyer and poet
    Author: "Florence Vane," 1840
            Froissart Ballad and Other Poems,
      1847
            various short stories

DELANY, Martin Robinson
    b. Charles Town, Va. (now Charleston, W. Va.,
        May 6, 1812
    d. January 24, 1885
    Originator and president National Emigra-
        tion Convention, 1854
    Appointed to lead expedition to Niger Valley,
        Africa to explore possibility of returning
        Blacks to the region
    Commanding major, U. S. Army - first
        Black major, 1865

Author: <u>Condition, Elevation and Destiny
of the Colored People of the United
States Politically Considered</u>, 1852

ELKINS, William Lukens
    b. May 2, 1832
    d. 1903
    Oil producer, 1861-75
    Partner, Standard Oil Co., 1875-80
    Sold out interests to Standard Oil Co.
      and purchased interests in gas
      plants throughout United States

JACKSON, Thomas Jonathan (Stonewall)
    b. Clarksburg, Va. (now W. Va.), January
      21, 1824
    d. Fredericksburg, Va., May 10, 1863
    Served in U. S. Army, Mexican War
    Professor of Artillery Tactics and Natural
      Philosophy, Virginia Military Insti-
      tute, 1851-61
    Commissioned brigadier general, Confederate
      Army, 1861, in command of Shenandoah
      Valley District, Department of Northern
      Virginia
    Fought at 2nd Battle of Bulls Run, Har-
      per's Ferry, Antietam, and Fredericks-
      burg

LUCAS, Robert
    b. Shepherdstown, Va. (now W. Va.),
      April 1, 1781
    d. Iowa City, February 7, 1853
    Member lower house, Ohio Legislature,
      1808-09, 1831-32
    Member Ohio Senate, 1814-22, 1824-28,
      1829-30
    Governor of Ohio, 1832-36
    First governor, superintendent Indian
      Affairs, Territory of Iowa, 1838-41

MILLER, John
    b. Berkeley County, Va. (now W. Va.), No-
      vember 25, 1781
    d. Florissant, Mo., March 18, 1846
    Served in War of 1812
    Governor of Missouri, 1825-32
    U. S. Representative (Missouri), 1837-43

MORROW, Dwight Whitney
    b. Huntington, W. Va., January 11, 1873
    d. October 5, 1931
    U. S. Ambassador to Mexico, 1927-31

Delegate to 6th Pan American Conference, 1928
Delegate to Naval Conference, London, England,
    1930

PAYNE, John Barton
    b. Pruntytown, Va. (now W. Va.), January
        26. 1855
    d. January 24, 1935
    Judge, Superior Court of Cook County, Ill.,
        1893-98
    General Counsel for U. S. Shipping Board
        Emergency Fleet Corporation, 1917-18
    General Counsel for U. S. Railroad Adminis-
        tration, 1917-19
    U. S. Secretary of the Interior, 1920-21

REUTHER, Walter P.
    b. Wheeling, W. Va., September 1, 1907
    d. May 9, 1970
    Began as apprentice tool and die maker,
        Wheeling, W. Va. Steel Corp., 1924
    Became President Local 194,
        United Automobile Workers, 1935
    President Aircraft and Agricultural Workers
        of America, CIO, 1946-70
    President, CIO, 1952-70
    President American Federation of Labor-
        Congress of Industrial Organizations,
        1955-70

SKIDMORE, Hubert Standish
    b. Webster Springs, W. Va., April 11, 1911
    d. February 2, 1946
    Author: I Will Lift Up Mine Eyes, 1936
            Heaven Came So Near, 1938
            River Rising, 1939

STRAUSS, Lewis Lichtenstein
    b. Charleston, W. Va., January 31, 1896
    Partner, Kuhn, Loeb and Co., 1929-47
    Member United States Atomic Energy Com-
        mission, 1946-50
    Special assistant to the President on Atomic
        Energy Matters, 1953
    Chairman, Atomic Energy Commission, 1953-58
    U. S. Secretary of Commerce, 1958-59
    Director Radio Corporation of America,
        National Broadcasting Company

VANCE, Cyrus R.
    b. Clarksburg, W. Va., March 27, 1917
    General counsel Department of Defense,
        1961-62

U. S. Secretary of the Army, 1962-63
U. S. Deputy Secretary of Defense, 1964-67
Special Representative of the President
    to Cyprus, 1967
Special Representative of the President to
    Korea, 1968
United States negotiator, Paris Peace Con-
    ference on Vietnam, 1968-69
U. S. Secretary of State, 1977-

WALDO, David
    b. Clarksburg, Va. (now W. Va.), April 30,
        1802
    d. Independence, Mo., May 20, 1878
    Practiced medicine, New Mexico
    Became Santa Fe trader, 1827
    Served Mexican War

WHITE, Israel Charles
    b. Monongalia County, W. Va., November 1,
        1848
    d. 1927
    Assistant Geologist, U. S. Geological Sur-
        vey, 1884-88
    State Geologist, West Virginia, 1897
    Specialist in coal, petroleum and
        natural gas - made many discoveries
    Member Federal Trade Commission

WORTHINGTON, Thomas
    b. Charles Town, Va. (W. Va,), July 16,
        1773
    d. New York, N. Y., June 20, 1827
    Member first Ohio Constitutional Convention,
        1802
    Member Ohio General Assembly, 1803
    U. S. Senator (Ohio), 1803-07
    Member Ohio General Assembly, 1807-08
    U. S. Senator (Ohio), 1810-14
    Governor of Ohio, 1814-18
    Member, Ohio House of Representatives,
        1821-23, 1824-25

FIRST STATE CONSTITUTION

CONSTITUTION OF WEST VIRGINIA—1861–1863 ª

ARTICLE I

THE STATE

SECTION 1. The State of West Virginia shall be and remain one of the United States of America. The Constitution of the United States, and the laws and treaties made in pursuance thereof, shall be the supreme law of the land.

SEC. 2. The following counties, formerly parts of the State of Virginia, shall be included in, and form a part of, the State of West Virginia, namely: the counties of Hancock, Brooke, Ohio, Marshall, Wetzel, Marion, Monongalia, Preston, Taylor, Pleasants, Tyler, Ritchie, Doddridge, Harrison, Wood, Jackson, Wirt, Roane, Calhoun, Gilmer, Barbour, Tucker, Lewis, Braxton, Upshur, Randolph, Mason, Putnam, Kanawha, Clay, Nicholas, Cabell, Wayne, Boone,

---

ª This constitution was framed by a convention which assembled at Wheeling November 26, 1861, and completed its labors February 18, 1862. It was submitted to the people of the counties named April 3, 1862, and the returns received showed its ratification by 28,321 votes against 572 votes. The consent of the body recognized by the Federal Government as the legislature of Virginia was given, and Congress then passed an act, approved December 31, 1862, providing for the admission of the new State, upon condition of the adoption of an amendment by the people represented in convention. This was done, and the State was admitted, with the amended constitution.

Logan, Wyoming, Mercer, McDowell, Webster, Pocahontas, Fayette, Raleigh, Greenbrier, and Monroe. And if a majority of the votes cast at the election or elections held, as provided in the schedule hereof, in the district composed of the counties of Pendleton, Hardy, Hampshire, and Morgan shall be in favor of the adoption of this constitution, the said four counties shall also be included in, and form part of, the State of West Virginia; and if the same shall be so included, and a majority of the votes cast at the said election or elections in the district composed of the counties of Berkeley, Jefferson, and Frederick shall be in favor of the adoption of this constitution, then the three last-mentioned counties shall also be included in, and form a part of, the State of West Virginia. The State of West Virginia shall also include so much of the bed, banks, and shores of the Ohio River as heretofore appertained to the State of Virginia, and the territorial rights and property in, and the jurisdiction of whatever nature over, the said bed, banks, and shores heretofore reserved by, or vested in, the State of Virginia shall vest in and be hereafter exercised by the State of West Virginia.

SEC. 3. The powers of government reside in all the citizens of the State, and can be rightfully exercised only in accordance with their will and appointment.

SEC. 4. The legislative, executive, and judicial departments of the government shall be separate and distinct. Neither shall exercise the powers properly belonging to either of the others. No person shall be invested with or exercise the powers of more than one of them at the same time.

SEC. 5. Writs, grants, and commissions, issued under State authority, shall run in the name of, and official bonds shall be made payable to; "the State of West Virginia." Indictments shall conclude, "against the peace and dignity of the State of West Virginia."

SEC. 6. The citizens of the State are the citizens of the United States residing therein; but no person in the military, naval, or marine service of the United States shall be deemed a resident of this State by reason of being stationed therein.

SEC. 7. Every citizen shall be entitled to equal representation in the government, and in all apportionments of representation, equality of numbers of those entitled thereto shail, as far as practicable, be preserved.

ARTICLE II

BILL OF RIGHTS

SECTION 1. The privilege of the writ of *habeas corpus* shall not be suspended, except when in time of invasion, insurrection, or other public danger the public safety may require it. No person shall be held to answer for treason, felony, or other crime not cognizable by a justice, unless on presentment or indictment of a grand jury. No bill of attainder, *ex post facto* law, or law impairing the obligation of a contract shall be passed.

SEC. 2. Excessive bail shall not be required, or excessive fines imposed, or cruel and unusual punishments inflicted. Penalties shall be proportioned to the character and degree of the offence. No person shall be compelled to be a witness against himself, or be twice put in jeopardy for the same offence.

SEC. 3. The right of the citizens to be secure in their houses, persons, papers, and effects against unreasonable searches and seizures shall not be violated. No warrant shall issue but upon probable cause, supported by oath or affirmation, and particularly describing the place to be searched, and the persons and things to be seized.

SEC. 4. No law abridging freedom of speech or of the press shall be passed; but the legislature may provide for the restraint and punishment of the publishing and vending of obscene books, papers, and pictures, and of libel and defamation of character, and for the recovery, in civil actions, by the aggrieved party, of suitable damages for such libel or defamation. Attempts to justify and uphold an armed invasion of the State, or an organized insurrection therein, during the continuance of such invasion or insurrection, by publicly speaking, writing, or printing, or by publishing or circulating such writing or printing, may be, by law, declared a misdemeanor, and punished accordingly.

SEC. 5. In prosecutions and civil suits for libel the truth may be given in evidence; and if it shall appear to the jury that the matter charged as libellous is true, and was published with good motives and for justifiable ends, the verdict shall be for the defendant.

SEC. 6. Private property shall not be taken for public use without just compensation. No person, in time of peace, shall be deprived of life, liberty, or property without due process of law. The military shall be subordinate to the civil power.

SEC. 7. In suits at common law, where the value in controversy exceeds twenty dollars, the right of trial by jury, if required by either party, shall be preserved. No fact tried by a jury shall be otherwise reëxamined in any case than according to the rules of the common law.

SEC. 8. The trial of crimes and misdemeanors, unless herein otherwise provided, shall be by jury, and shall be held publicly and without unreasonable delay, in the county where the alleged offence was committed, unless upon petition of the accused and for good cause shown, or in consequence of the existence of war or insurrection in such county, it is removed to, or instituted in, some other county. In all such trials the accused shall be informed of the character and cause of the accusation, and be confronted with the witnesses against him, and shall have the assistance of counsel for his defence, and compulsory process for obtaining witnesses in his favor.

SEC. 9. No man shall be compelled to frequent or support any religious worship, place, or ministry whatsoever; nor shall any man be enforced, restrained, molested, or burdened in his body or goods, or otherwise suffer, on account of his religious belief; but all men shall be free to profess, and by argument to maintain, their opinions in matters of religion, and the same shall in no wise affect, diminish, or enlarge their civil capacities. And the legislature shall not prescribe any religious test whatever; or confer any peculiar privileges or advantages on any sect or denomination; or pass any law requiring or authorizing any religious society, or the people of any district within this State, to levy on themselves or others any tax for the erection or repair of any house for public worship, or for the support of any church or ministry; but it shall be left free to every person to select his religious instructor, and to make for his support such private contract as he shall please.

SEC. 10. Treason against the State shall consist only in levying war against it, or in adhering to its enemies, giving them aid and comfort. No person shall be convicted of treason unless on the testimony of two witnesses to the same overt act, or on confession in open court. Treason shall be punished, according to the character of the acts committed, by the infliction of one or more of the penalties of death, imprisonment, fine, or confiscation of the real and personal property of the offender, as may be prescribed by law.

ARTICLE III

ELECTIONS AND OFFICERS

SECTION 1. The white male citizens of the State shall be entitled to vote at all elections held within the election districts in which they respectively reside; but no person who is a minor, or of unsound mind, or a pauper, or who is under conviction of treason, felony, or bribery in an election, or who has not been a resident of the State for one year, and of the county in which he offers to vote for thirty days, next preceding such offer, shall be permitted to vote while such disability continues.[a]

SEC. 2. In all elections by the people, the mode of voting shall be by ballot.

SEC. 3. No voter during the continuance of an election at which he is entitled to vote, or during the time necessary and convenient for going to and returning from the same, shall be subject to arrest upon civil process, or be liable to attend any court or judicial proceeding as suitor, juror, or witness; or to work upon the public roads; or, except in time of war or public danger, to render military service.

SEC. 4. No persons, except citizens entitled to vote, shall be elected or appointed to any State, county, or municipal office. Judges must have attained the age of thirty-five years, the governor the age of thirty years, and the attorney-general and senators the age of twenty-five years, at the beginning of their respective terms of service, and must have been citizens of the State for five years next preceding, or at the time this constitution goes into operation.

SEC. 5. Every person elected or appointed to any office or trust, civil or military, shall, before proceeding to exercise the authority or discharge the duties of the same, make oath or affirmation that he will support the Constitution of the United States, and the constitution of this State; and every citizen of this State may, in time of war, insurrection, or public danger, be required by law to make like oath or affirmation, upon pain of suspension of his right of voting and holding office under this constitution.

SEC. 6. All officers elected or appointed under this constitution may be removed from office for misconduct, incompetence, neglect of duty, or other causes, in such manner as may be prescribed by general laws; and unless so removed, shall continue to discharge the duties of their respective offices until their successors are elected or appointed and qualified.

---

[a] See amendment.

Sec. 7. The general elections of State and county officers, and of members of the legislature, shall be held on the fourth Thursday of October. The terms of such officers and members, not elected or appointed to fill a vacancy, shall, unless herein otherwise provided, begin on the first day of January next succeeding their election. Elections to fill vacancies shall be for the unexpired term. Vacancies shall be filled in such manner as may be prescribed by law.

Sec. 8. The legislature, in cases not provided for in this constitution, shall prescribe by general laws the terms of office, powers, duties, and compensation of all public officers and agents, and the manner in which they shall be elected, appointed, and removed.

Sec. 9. No extra compensation shall be granted or allowed to any public officer, agent, or contractor, after the services shall have been rendered, or the contract entered into. Nor shall the salary or compensation of any public officer be increased or diminished during his term of office.

Sec. 10. Any officer of the State may be impeached for maladministration, corruption, incompetence, neglect of duty, or any high crime or misdemeanor. The house of delegates shall have the sole power of impeachment. The senate shall have the sole power to try impeachments. When sitting for that purpose, the senators shall be on oath or affirmation; and no person shall be convicted without the concurrence of two-thirds of the members present. Judgment in cases of impeachment shall not extend further than to removal from office and disqualification to hold any office of honor, trust, or profit under the State; but the party convicted shall, nevertheless, be liable and subject to indictment, trial, judgment, and punishment according to law. The senate may sit during the recess of the legislature, for the trial of impeachments.

Sec. 11. Any citizen of this State, who shall, after the adoption of this constitution, either in or out of the State, fight a duel with deadly weapons, or send or accept a challenge so to do; or who shall act as a second, or knowingly aid or assist in such duel, shall ever thereafter be incapable of holding any office of honor, trust, or profit under this State.

Sec. 12. The legislature may provide for a registry of voters. They shall prescribe the manner of conducting and making returns of elections, and of determining contested elections; and shall pass such laws as may be necessary and proper to prevent intimidation, disorder, or violence at the polls, and corruption or fraud in voting.

ARTICLE IV

LEGISLATURE

Section 1. The legislative power shall be vested in a senate and house of delegates. The style of their acts shall be, " *Be it enacted by the legislature of West Virginia.*"

Sec. 2. The senate shall be composed of eighteen, and the house of delegates of forty-seven members, subject to be increased according to the provisions hereinafter contained.

Sec. 3. The term of office of senators shall be two years, and that of delegates one year. The senators first elected shall divide themselves into two classes, one senator from every district being assigned to each class; and of these classes, the first, to be designated by lot in such manner as the senate may determine, shall hold their offices for one year, and the second for two years; so that after the first election one-half of the senators shall be elected annually.

SEC. 4. For the election of senators, the State shall be divided into nine senatorial districts, which number shall not be diminished, but may be increased as hereinafter provided. Every district shall choose two senators, but after the first election both shall not be chosen from the same county. The districts shall be equal, as nearly as practicable, in white population, according to the returns of the United States census. They shall be compact, formed of contiguous territory, and bounded by county lines. After every such census the legislature shall alter the senatorial districts, so far as may be necessary to make them conform to the foregoing provisions.

SEC. 5. Any senatorial district may at any time be divided by county lines or otherwise, into two sections, which shall be equal, as nearly as practicable, in white population. If such division be made, each section shall elect one of the senators for the district; and the senators so elected shall be classified in such manner as the senate may determine.

SEC. 6. Until the senatorial districts are altered by the legislature after the next census, the counties of Hancock, Brooke, and Ohio shall constitute the first senatorial district; Marshall, Wetzell, and Marion the second; Monongalia, Preston, and Taylor the third; Pleasants, Tyler, Ritchie, Doddridge, and Harrison the fourth; Wood, Jackson, Wirt, Roane, Calhoun, and Gilmer the fifth; Barbour, Tucker, Lewis, Braxton, Upshur, and Randolph the sixth; Mason, Putnam, Kanawha, Clay, and Nicholas the seventh; Cabell, Wayne, Boone, Logan, Wyoming, Mercer, and McDowell the eighth; and Webster, Pocahontas, Fayette, Raleigh, Greenbrier, and Monroe the ninth.

SEC. 7. For the election of delegates, every county containing a white population of less than half the ratio of representation for the house of delegates, shall, at each apportionment, be attached to some contiguous county or counties, to form a delegate district.

SEC. 8. When two or more counties are formed into a delegate district, the legislature shall provide by law that the delegates to be chosen by the voters of the district shall be in rotation, residents of each county, for a greater or less number of terms, proportioned as nearly as can be conveniently done to the white population of the several counties in the district.

SEC. 9. After every census the delegates shall be apportioned as follows:

The ratio of representation for the house of delegates shall be ascertained by dividing the whole white population of the State by the number of which the house is to consist and rejecting the fraction of a unit, if any, resulting from such division.

Dividing the white population of every delegate district, and of every county not included in a delegate district, by the ratio thus ascertained, there shall be assigned to each a number of delegates equal to the quotient obtained by this division, excluding the fractional remainder.

The additional delegates necessary to make up the number of which the house is to consist shall then be assigned to those delegate districts and counties not included in a delegate district, which would otherwise have the largest fractions unrepresented. But every delegate district and county not included in a delegate district shall be entitled to at least one delegate.

SEC. 10. Until a new apportionment is declared, the counties of Pleasants and Wood shall form the first delegate district; Calhoun and Gilmer the second; Clay and Nicholas the third; Webster and Pocahontas the fourth; Tucker and Randolph the fifth; and McDowell, Wyoming, and Raleigh the sixth. The first delegate district shall choose two delegates, and the other five one each.

SEC. 11. The delegates to be chosen by the first delegate district shall, for the first term, both be residents of the county of Wood, and for the second term, one shall be a resident of Wood, and the other of Pleasants County; and so in rotation. The delegate to be chosen by the second delegate district shall, for the first term, be a resident of Gilmer, and for the second of Calhoun County. The delegate to be chosen by the third delegate district shall, for the first two terms, be a resident of Nicholas, and for the third term of Clay County. The delegate to be chosen by the fourth delegate district shall, for the first two terms, be a resident of Pocahontas, and for the third term of Webster County. The delegate to be chosen by the fifth delegate district shall, for the first three terms, be a resident of Randolph, and for the fourth term of Tucker County. And the delegate to be chosen by the sixth delegate district shall, for the first term, be a resident of Raleigh, for the second term of Wyoming, for the third term of Raleigh, for the fourth term of Wyoming, and for the fifth term of McDowell County; and so, in each case, in rotation.

SEC. 12. Until a new apportionment is declared, the apportionment of delegates to the counties not included in delegate districts shall be as follows:

To Barbour, Boone, Braxton, Brooke, Cabell, Doddridge, Fayette, Hancock, Jackson, Lewis, Logan, Mason, Mercer, Putnam, Ritchie, Roane, Taylor, Tyler, Upshur, Wayne, Wetzel, and Wirt Counties, one delegate each.

To Harrison, Kanawha, Marion, Marshall, Monongalia, and Preston Counties, two delegates each.

To Ohio County, three delegates.

To Greenbrier and Monroe Counties together, three delegates: of whom, for the first term, two shall be residents of Greenbrier and one of Monroe County; and for the second term, two shall be residents of Monroe and one of Greenbrier County; and so in rotation.

SEC. 13. If the counties of Pendleton, Hardy, Hampshire, and Morgan become part of this State, they shall, until the next apportionment, constitute the tenth senatorial district, and choose two senators. And if the counties of Frederick, Berkeley, and Jefferson becomes part of this State, they shall, until the next apportionment, constitute the eleventh senatorial district and choose two senators. And the number of the senate shall be, in the first case, twenty, and in the last twenty-two, instead of eighteen.

SEC. 14. If the seven last-named counties become part of this State, the apportionment of delegates to the same shall, until the next apportionment, be as follows: To Pendleton and Hardy, one each; to Hampshire, Frederick, and Jefferson, two each; and the counties of Morgan and Berkeley shall form the seventh delegate district, and choose two delegates; of whom, for the first term, one shall be a resident of Berkeley and the other of Morgan County; and for the second term, both shall be residents of Berkeley County; and so in rotation.

But if the counties of Pendleton, Hardy, Hampshire, and Morgan become part of the State, and Frederick, Berkeley, and Jefferson do not, then Pendleton, Hardy, and Morgan Counties shall each choose one delegate, and Hampshire two, until the next apportionment.

The number of the house of delegates shall, instead of forty-seven, be in the first case fifty-seven, and in the last, fifty-two.

SEC. 15. The arrangement of senatorial and delegate districts, and appointment of delegates, shall hereafter be declared by law, as soon as possible after each succeeding census taken by authority of the United States. When so declared, they shall apply to the first general election for members of the legislature to be thereafter held, and shall continue in force unchanged until such districts are altered and delegates apportioned under the succeeding census.

SEC. 16. Additional territory may be admitted into and become part of this State with the consent of the legislature. And in such case provision shall be made by law for the representation of the white population thereof in the senate and house of delegates, in conformity with the principles set forth in this constitution. And the number of members of which each branch of the legislature is to consist shall thereafter be increased by the representation assigned to such additional territory.

SEC. 17. No person shall be a member of the legislature who shall not have resided within the district or county for which he was chosen one year next preceding his election; and if a senator or delegate remove from the district or county for which he was chosen, his office shall be thereby vacated.

SEC. 18. No person holding an office of profit under this State or the United States shall be a member of the legislature.

SEC. 19. No person who may have collected or been entrusted with public money, whether State, county, township, or municipal, shall be eligible to the legislature, or to any office of honor, trust, or profit, until he shall have duly accounted for and paid over such money according to law.

SEC. 20. The legislature shall meet once in every year, and not oftener, unless convened by the governor. The regular sessions shall begin on the third Tuesday of January.

SEC. 21. The governor may convene the legislature, by proclamation, whenever, in his opinion, the public safety or welfare shall require it. It shall be his duty to convene them on application of a majority of the members elected to each branch.

SEC. 22. The seat of government shall be at the city of Wheeling until a permanent seat of government be established by law.

SEC. 23. When, for any cause, the legislature, in the opinion of the governor, cannot safely meet at the seat of government, the governor, by proclamation, may convene them at another place.

Sec. 24. No session of the legislature, after the first, shall continue longer than forty-five days, without the concurrence of three-fourths of the members elected to each branch.

Sec. 25. Neither branch, during the session, shall adjourn for more than two days without the consent of the other. Nor shall either, without such consent, adjourn to any other place than that in which the legislature is then sitting.

Sec. 26. Each branch shall be the judge of the elections, qualifications, and returns of its own members.

Sec. 27. A majority of each branch shall constitute a quorum to do business. But a smaller number may adjourn from day to day, and compel the attendance of absent members, in such manner as shall be prescribed by law.

Sec. 28. The senate shall choose from their own body a president, and the house of delegates one of their own number as speaker. Each branch shall appoint its own officers and remove them at pleasure, and shall determine its own rules of proceeding.

Sec. 29. Each branch may punish its own members for disorderly behavior; and, with the concurrence of two-thirds of the members present, expel a member, but not a second time for the same offence.

Sec. 30. Each branch shall have the power necessary to provide for its own safety, and the undisturbed transaction of its business, and may punish, by imprisonment, any person, not a member, for disrespectful behavior in its presence, obstructing any of its proceedings, or any of its officers in the discharge of his duties; or for any assault, threatening, or abuse of a member for words spoken in debate. But such imprisonment shall not extend beyond the termination of the session, and shall not prevent the punishment of any offence by the ordinary course of law.

Sec. 31. For words spoken in debate, or any report, motion, or proposition made, in either branch, a member shall not be questioned in any other place.

Sec. 32. Members of the legislature shall, in all cases except treason, felony, and breach of the peace, be privileged from arrest during the session, and for ten days before and after the same.

Sec. 33. Senators and delegates shall receive for their services a compensation not exceeding three dollars a day during the session of the legislature, and also ten cents for every mile they shall travel in going to and returning from the place of meeting by the most direct route. The president of the senate and speaker of the house shall, respectively, receive an additional compensation of two dollars a day.

Sec. 34. Bills and resolutions may originate in either branch, to be passed, amended, or rejected by the other.

Sec. 35. No bill shall become a law until it has been fully and distinctly read on three different days in each branch, unless, in cases of urgency, three-fourths of the members present dispense with this rule.

Sec. 36. No law shall embrace more than one object, which shall be expressed in its title.

Sec. 37. On the passage of every bill, the vote shall be taken by yeas and nays, and be entered on the journal; and no bill shall be passed by either branch without the affirmative vote of a majority of the members elected thereto.

Sec. 38. The presiding officer of each branch shall sign, before the close of the session, all bills and joint resolutions passed by the legislature.

Sec. 39. Each branch shall keep a journal of its proceeding, and cause the same to be published from time to time; and the yeas and nays on any question, if called for by one-fifth of those present, shall be entered on the journal.

Article V

EXECUTIVE

Section 1. The chief executive power shall be vested in a governor, who shall be elected by the voters of the State, and hold his office for the term of two years, to commence on the fourth day of March next succeeding his election. The person acting as governor shall not be elected or appointed to any other office during his term of service.

Sec. 2. The governor shall reside at the seat of government; shall receive two thousand dollars for each year of his service, and, during his continuance in office, shall receive no other emolument from this or any other government.

Sec. 3. The governor shall be commander-in-chief of the military forces of the State; shall have power to call out the militia to repel invasion, suppress insurrection, and enforce the execution of the laws; shall conduct in person, or in such manner as may be prescribed by law, all intercourse with other States; and, during the recess of the legislature, shall fill temporarily all vacancies in office, not provided for by this constitution or the legislature, by commissions to expire at the end of thirty days after the commencement of the succeeding session of the legislature. He shall take care that the laws be faithfully executed; communicate to the legislature at each session thereof the condition of the State, and recommend to their consideration such measures as he may deem expedient. He shall have power to remit fines and penalties in such cases and under such regulations as may be prescribed by law; to commute capital punishment, and, except when the prosecution has been carried on by the house of delegates, to grant reprieves and pardons after conviction; but he shall communicate to the legislature, at each session, the particulars of every case of fine or penalty remitted, of punishment commuted, and of reprieve or pardon granted, with his reasons for remitting, commuting, or granting the same.

Sec. 4. The governor may require information in writing from the officers of the executive department, upon any subject pertaining to their respective offices, and also the opinion in writing of the attorney-general upon any question of law relating to the business of the executive department.

Sec. 5. Returns of the election of governor shall be made, in the manner and by the persons designated by the legislature, to the secretary of the State, who shall deliver them to the speaker of the house of delegates on the first day of the next session of the legislature. The speaker shall, within ten days thereafter, in the presence of a majority of each branch of the legislature, open the said returns, when the votes shall be counted. The person having the highest number of votes, if duly qualified, shall be declared elected; but if two or more have the highest and an equal number of votes, one of them shall thereupon be chosen governor by the joint vote of the two branches. Contested elections for governor shall be decided by a like vote, and the mode of proceeding in such cases shall be prescribed by law.

SEC. 6. In case of the removal of the governor from office, or of his death, failure to qualify within the time prescribed by law, resignation, removal from the seat of government, or inability to discharge the duties of the office, the said office, with its compensation, duties, and authority, shall devolve upon the president of the senate; and in case of his inability or failure from any cause to act, on the speaker of the house of delegates. The legislature shall provide by law for the discharge of the executive functions in other necessary cases.

SEC. 7. A secretary of state, a treasurer, and an auditor shall be elected at the same time and for the same term as the governor. Their duties shall be prescribed by law. The secretary of the State shall receive thirteen hundred, the treasurer fourteen hundred, and the auditor fifteen hundred dollars per annum.

SEC. 8. The governor shall nominate and, by and with the advice and consent of the senate, appoint all military officers above the rank of colonel.

ARTICLE VI

JUDICIARY

SECTION 1. The judicial power of the State shall be vested in a supreme court of appeals and circuit courts, and such inferior tribunals as are herein authorized.

SEC. 2. The State shall be divided into nine circuits. The counties of Hancock, Brooke, Ohio, and Marshall shall constitute the first; Monongalia, Preston, Tucker, and Taylor the second; Marion. Harrison, and Barbour the third; Wetzel, Tyler, Pleasants, Ritchie, Doddridge, and Gilmer the fourth; Randolph, Upshur, Calhoun, Roane, Jackson, and Clay the sixth; Kanawha, Mason, Putnam, and Fayette the seventh; Cabell, Wayne, Boone, Logan, Wyoming, and Raleigh the eighth; and Pocahontas, Greenbrier. Monroe, Mercer, and McDowell the ninth. If the counties of Pendleton, Hardy, Hampshire, and Morgan become a part of the State, they shall constitute another circuit, to be called the tenth. And if the counties of Frederick. Berkeley, and Jefferson become a part of this State, they shall constitute the eleventh circuit.

SEC. 3. The legislature may, from time to time, rearrange the circuits; and after the expiration of five years from the time this constitution goes into operation, and thereafter, at periods of ten years. may increase or diminish the number of circuits, or the number of courts in a year, as necessity may require.

SEC. 4. For each circuit a judge shall be elected by the voters thereof, who shall hold his office for the term of six years. During his continuance in office he shall reside in the circuit of which he is judge.

SEC. 5. A circuit court shall be held in every county at least four times a year, unless otherwise provided by law, in pursuance of the third section of this article. The judges may be required or authorized to hold the courts of their respective circuits alternately, and a judge of one circuit to hold a court in any other circuit.

Sec. 6. The circuit courts shall have the supervision and control of all proceedings before justices and other inferior tribunals, by *mandamus*, prohibition, or *certiorari*. They shall, except in cases confined exclusively by this constitution to some other tribunal, have original and general jurisdiction of all matters at law, where the amount in controversy, exclusive of interest, exceeds twenty dollars, and of all cases in equity, and of all crimes and misdemeanors. They shall have appellate jurisdiction in all cases, civil and criminal, weher an appeal, writ of error, or *supersedeas* may be allowed to the judgment or proceedings of any inferior tribunal. They shall also have such other jurisdiction, whether supervisory, original, appellate, or concurrent, as may be prescribed by law.

Sec. 7. The supreme court of appeals shall consist of three judges, any two of whom shall be a quorum. They shall be elected by the voters of the State, and shall hold their offices for the term of twelve years; except that of those first elected, one, to be designated by lot in such manner as they may determine, shall hold his office for four years; another, to be designated in like manner, for eight years, and the third for twelve years; so that one shall be elected every four years after the first election.

Sec. 8. The supreme court of appeals shall have original jurisdiction in cases of *habeas corpus*, *mandamus*, and prohibition. It shall have appellate jurisdiction in civil cases where the matter in controversy, exclusive of costs, is of greater value or amount than two hundred dollars; in controversies concerning the title or boundaries of land, the probate of wills, the appointment or qualification of a personal representative, guardian, committee, or curator, or concerning a mill, road, way, ferry, or landing, or the right of a corporation or county to levy tolls or taxes; and also in cases of *habeas corpus*, *mandamus*, and prohibition, and cases involving freedom, or the constitutionality of a law. It shall have appellate jurisdiction in criminal cases where there has been a conviction for felony or misdemeanor in a circuit court, and such other appellate jurisdiction in both civil and criminal cases as may be prescribed by law.

Sec. 9. When a judgment or decree is reversed or affirmed by the supreme court of appeals, every point made and distinctly stated in writing in the cause, and fairly arising upon the record of the case, shall be considered and decided, and the reasons therefor shall be concisely and briefly stated in writing, and preserved with the records of the case.

Sec. 10. When any judge of the court of appeals is so situated in regard to any case pending before it as to make it improper for him to aid in the trial of the same, or is under any other disability, the remaining judges may call to their assistance a judge of the circuit court, who shall act as a judge of the court of appeals in the cases to which such disability relates.

Sec. 11. Judges shall be commissioned by the governor. The salary of a judge of the supreme court of appeals shall be two thousand, and that of a judge of a circuit court eighteen hundred dollars per annum, and each shall receive the same allowance for necessary travel as members of the legislature.

Sec. 12. No judge, during his term of office, shall hold any other office, appointment, or public trust, under this or any other government, and the acceptance thereof shall vacate his judicial office; nor shall he, during his continuance therein, be eligible to any political office.

Sec. 13. Judges may be removed from office for misconduct, incompetence, or neglect of duty, or on conviction of an infamous offence, by the concurrent vote of a majority of all the members elected to each branch of the legislature, and the cause of removal shall be entered on the journals. The judge against whom the legislature may be about to proceed shall receive notice thereof, accompanied by a copy of the causes alleged for his removal, at least twenty days before the day on which either branch of the legislature shall act thereon.

Sec. 14. The officers of the supreme court of appeals shall be appointed by the court, or by the judges thereof in vacation. Their duties, compensation, and tenure of office shall be prescribed by law.

Sec. 15. The voters of each county shall elect a clerk of the circuit court, whose term of office shall be four years. His duties and compensation, and the mode of removing him from office, shall be prescribed by law; and when a vacancy shall occur in the office, the judge of the circuit court shall appoint a clerk, who shall discharge the duties of the office until the vacancy is filled. In any case, in respect to which the clerk shall be so situated as to make it improper for him to act, the court shall appoint a substitute.

Sec. 16. At every regular election of a governor, an attorney-general shall be elected. He shall be commissioned by the governor; shall perform such duties and receive such compensation as may be prescribed by law, and be removable in the same manner as the judges.

Sec. 17. The legislature may establish courts of limited jurisdiction within any incorporated town or city, subject to appeal to the circuit courts.

Article VII

COUNTIES AND TOWNSHIPS

Section 1. Every county shall be divided into not less than three nor more than ten townships, laid off as compactly as practicable, with reference to natural boundaries, and containing, as nearly as practicable, an equal number of white population, but not less than four hundred. Each township shall be designated, " The township of ———, in the county of ———," by which name it may sue and be sued.

Sec. 2. The voters of each township, assembled in stated or special township meeting, shall transact all such business relating exclusively to their township as is herein, or may be by law, required or authorized. They shall annually elect a supervisor, clerk of the township, surveyor of roads for each precinct in their township, overseer of the poor, and such other officers as may be directed by law. They shall also, every four years, elect one justice, and if the white population of their township exceeds twelve hundred in number, may elect an additional justice; and every two years shall elect as many constables as justices. The supervisor, or, in his absence, a voter chosen by those present, shall preside at all township meetings and elections, and the clerk shall act as clerk thereof.

SEC. 3. The supervisors chosen in the townships of each county
shall constitute a board to be known as " the supervisors of the county
of ———," by which name they may sue and be sued, and make and
use a common seal, and enact ordinances and by-laws not inconsistent
with the laws of the State. They shall meet statedly, at least four
times in each year, at the court-house of their county, and may hold
special and adjourned meetings. At their first meeting after the
annual township election, and whenever a vacancy may occur, they
shall elect one of their number president of the board, and appoint a
clerk, who shall keep a journal of their proceedings, and transact
such other business pertaining to his office as may be by them or by
law required, and whose compensation they shall fix by ordinance
and pay from the county treasury.

SEC. 4. The board of supervisors of each county, a majority of
whom shall be a quorum, shall, under such general regulations as may
be prescribed by law, have the superintendence and administration of
the internal affairs and fiscal concerns of their county, including the
establishment and regulation of roads, public landings, ferries, and
mills; the granting of ordinary and other licenses; and the laying,
collecting, and disbursement of the county levies; but all writs of
ad quod damnum shall issue from the circuit courts. They shall from
time to time appoint the places for holding elections in the several
townships of their county; and shall be the judges of the election,
qualifications, and returns of their own members, and of all county
and township officers.

SEC. 5. The voters of every county shall elect a sheriff, prosecuting
attorney, surveyor of lands, recorder, one or more assessors, and such
other county officers as the legislature may from time to time direct
or authorize; the duties of all of whom shall be prescribed and defined, as far as practicable, by general laws. All the said county
officers shall hold their offices for two years, except the sheriff, whose
term of office shall be four years. The same person shall not be
elected sheriff for two consecutive full terms, nor shall any person who
has acted as deputy of any sheriff be elected his successor, nor shall
any sheriff act as the deputy of his successor; but the retiring sheriff
shall finish all business remaining in his hands at the expiration of his
term, for which purpose his commission and official bond shall continue in force. The duties of all the said officers shall be discharged
by the incumbents thereof in person, or under their superintendence.
The board of supervisors shall designate one or more constables of
their respective counties to serve process and levy executions, when
the sheriff thereof is a party defendant in a suit instituted therein,
or is under any other disability.

SEC. 6. The recorder, in addition to the duties incident to the
recording of inventories, and other papers relating to estates, and
deeds and other writings, the registering of births, marriages, and
deaths, and the issuing of marriage licenses, shall have authority,
under such regulations as may be prescribed by law, to receive proof
of wills and admit them to probate, to appoint and qualify personal
representatives, guardians, committees, and curators, to administer
oaths, take acknowledgments of deeds and other writings, and relin-
quishments of dower.

SEC. 7. The legislature shall, at their first session, by general laws,
provide for carrying into effect the foregoing provisions of this

article. They shall also provide for commissioning such of the officers therein mentioned as they may deem proper, and may require any class of them to give bond with security for the faithful discharge of the duties of their respective offices, and for accounting for and paying over, as required by law, all money which may come to their hands by virtue thereof. They shall further provide for the compensation of the said officers by fees, or from the county treasury; and for the appointment, when necessary, of deputies and assistants, whose duties and responsibilities shall be prescribed and defined by general laws. When the compensation of an officer is paid from the county treasury, the amounts shall be fixed by the board of supervisors, within limits to be ascertained by law.

Sec. 8. The civil jurisdiction of a justice shall extend to actions of assumpsit, debt, detinue, and trover, if the amount claimed, exclusive of interest, does not exceed one hundred dollars, when the defendant resides, or, being a non-resident of the State, is found, or has effects or estate within his township, or when the cause of action arose therein; but any other justice of the same county may issue a summons to the defendant to appear before the justice of the proper township, which may be served by a constable of either township. In case of a vacancy in the office of justice or constable in any township having but one, or of the disability to act of the incumbent, any other justice or constable of the same county may discharge the duties of their respective offices within the said township. The manner of conducting the aforesaid actions, and of issuing summonses and executions, and of executing and making return of the same, shall be prescribed by law; and the legislature may give to justices and constables such additional civil jurisdiction and powers, within their respective townships, as may be deemed expedient.

Sec. 9. Every justice and constable shall be a conservator of the peace throughout his county, and have such jurisdiction and powers in criminal cases therein as may be prescribed by law. Jurisdiction of all misdemeanors and breaches of the peace, punishable by fine not exceeding ten dollars, or by imprisonment for not more than thirty days, may be, by law, vested in the justices.

Sec. 10. Either party to a civil suit brought before a justice, where the value in controversy or the damages claimed exceeds twenty dollars, and the defendant in such cases of misdemeanor or breach of the peace as may be made by law cognizable by a single justice, when the penalty is imprisonment or a fine exceeding five dollars, shall be entitled to a trial by six jurors, if demanded, under such regulations as may be prescribed by law.

Sec. 11. In all cases an appeal shall lie, under such regulations as may be prescribed by law, from the judgment or proceedings of a justice or recorder, to the circuit court of the county, excepting judgments of justices in assumpsit, debt, detinue, and trover, and for fines, where the amount does not exceed ten dollars, exclusive of interest and costs, and where the case does not involve the freedom of a person, the validity of a law, or the right of corporation or county to levy tolls or taxes.

Sec. 12. No new county shall be formed having an area of less than four hundred square miles; or if another be thereby reduced below that area; or if any territory be thereby taken from a county containing less than four hundred square miles. And no new county shall be formed containing a white population of less than four thousand; or if the white population of another county be thereby reduced below that number; or if any county containing less than four thousand white inhabitants be thereby reduced in area. But the legislature may, at any time, annex any county containing less than four thousand white inhabitants to an adjoining county or counties as a part thereof.

SEC. 13. The board of supervisors may alter the bounds of a township of their county, or erect new townships therein, with the consent of a majority of the voters of each township interested, assembled in stated township meeting or in a meeting duly called for the purpose, subject to the provisions of the first section of this article.

SEC. 14. Nothing contained in this article shall impair or affect the charter of any municipal corporation, or restrict the power of the legislature to create or regulate such corporations.

ARTICLE VIII

TAXATION AND FINANCE

SECTION 1. Taxation shall be equal and uniform throughout the State, and all property, both real and personal, shall be taxed in proportion to its value, to be ascertained as directed by law. No one species of property from which a tax may be collected shall be taxed higher than any other species of property of equal value; but property used for educational, literary, scientific, religious, or charitable purposes, and public property, may, by law, be exempted from taxation.

SEC. 2. A capitation-tax of one dollar shall be levied upon each white male inhabitant who has attained the age of twenty-one years.

SEC. 3. The legislature shall provide for an annual tax, sufficient to defray the estimated expenses of the State for each year; and, whenever the ordinary expenses of any year shall exceed the income, shall levy a tax for the ensuing year, sufficient, with other sources of income, to pay the deficiency, as well as the estimated expenses of such year.

SEC. 4. No money shall be drawn from the treasury but in pursuance of appropriations made by law, and an accurate and detailed statement of the receipts and expenditures of the public money shall be published annually.

SEC. 5. No debt shall be contracted by this State, except to meet casual deficits in the revenue, to redeem a previous liability of the State, to suppress insurrection, repel invasion, or defend the State in time of war.

SEC. 6. The credit of the State shall not be granted to or in aid of any county, city, town, township, corporation, or person, nor shall the State ever assume or become responsible for the debts or liabilities of any county, city, town, township, corporation, or person, unless incurred in time of war or insurrection for the benefit of the State.

SEC. 7. The legislature may at any time direct a sale of the stocks owned by the State in banks and other corporations, but the proceeds of such sale shall be applied to the liquidation of the public debt; and hereafter the State shall not become a stockholder in any bank.

If the State become a stockholder in any association or corporation for purposes of internal improvement, such stock shall be paid for at the time of subscribing, or a tax shall be levied for the ensuing year, sufficient to pay the subscription in full.

SEC. 8. An equitable proportion of the public debt of the commonwealth of Virginia prior to the first day of January, in the year one thousand eight hundred and sixty-one, shall be assumed by this State; and the legislature shall ascertain the same as soon as may be practicable, and provide for the liquidation thereof, by a sinking-fund sufficient to pay the accruing interest and redeem the principal within thirty-four years.

ARTICLE IX

FORFEITED AND UNAPPROPRIATED LANDS

SECTION 1. All private rights and interests in lands in this State, derived from or under the laws of the State of Virginia prior to the time this constitution goes into operation, shall remain valid and secure, and shall be determined by the laws heretofore in force in the State of Virginia.

SEC. 2. No entry by warrant on land in this State shall be hereafter made; and in all cases where an entry has been heretofore made and has been or shall be so perfected as to entitle the locator to a grant, the legislature shall make provision by law for issuing the same.

SEC. 3. The legislature shall provide for the sale of all lands in this State heretofore forfeited to the State of Virginia for the non-payment of the taxes charged thereon for the year one thousand eight hundred and thirty-one, or any year previous thereto, or for the failure of the former owners to have the same entered on the land-books of the proper county and charged with the taxes due thereon for the said or any year previous thereto, under the laws of the State of Virginia, and also of all waste and unappropriated lands, by proceedings in the circuit courts of the county where such lands are situated.

SEC. 4. All lands within this State, returned delinquent for non-payment of taxes to the State of Virginia since the year one thousand eight hundred and thirty-one, where the taxes, exclusive of damages, do not exceed twenty dollars; and all lands forfeited for the failure of the owners to have the same entered on the land-books of the proper county, and charged with the taxes chargeable thereon since the year one thousand eight hundred and thirty-one, where the tract does not contain more than one thousand acres, are hereby released and exonerated from forfeiture and from the delinquent taxes and damages charged thereon.

SEC. 5. All lands in this State heretofore vested in the State of Virginia by forfeiture, or by purchase at the sheriffs' sales for delinquent taxes, and not released or exonerated by the laws thereof, or by the operation of the preceding section, may be redeemed by the former owners by payment to this State of the amount of taxes and damages due thereon at the time of such redemption, within five years form the day this constitution goes into operation; and all such lands not so released, exonerated, or redeemed shall be treated as forfeited, and proceeded against and sold as provided in the third section of this article.

SEC. 6. The former owner of any tract of land in this State sold under the provisions of this article shall be entitled to receive the excess of the sum for which such tract may be sold over the taxes and damages charged and chargeable thereon, and the costs, if his claim be filed in the circuit court which decreed the sale, within two years thereafter.

ARTICLE X

EDUCATION

SECTION 1. All money accruing to this State, being the proceeds of forfeited, delinquent, waste, and unappropriated lands, and of lands heretofore sold for taxes and purchased by the State of Virginia, if hereafter redeemed, or sold to others than this State; all grants, devises, or bequests that may be made to this State for the purposes of education, or where the purposes of such grants, devises, or bequests are not specified; this State's just share of the literary fund of Virginia, whether paid over or otherwise liquidated, and any sums of money, stocks, or property which this State shall have the right to claim from the State of Virginia for educational purposes; the proceeds of the estates of all persons who may die without leaving a will or heir, and of all escheated lands; the proceeds of any taxes that may be levied on the revenues of any corporation hereafter created; all moneys that may be paid as an equivalent for exemption from military duty, and such sums as may from time to time be appropriated by the legislature for the purpose, shall be set apart as a separate fund, to be called the school-fund, and invested under such regulations as may be prescribed by law, in the interest-bearing securities of the United States, or of this State, and the interest thereof shall be annually applied to the support of free schools throughout the State, and to no other purpose whatever. But any portion of said interest remaining unexpended at the close of the fiscal year shall be added to and remain a part of the capital of the school-fund.

SEC. 2. The legislature shall provide, as soon as practicable, for the establishment of a thorough and efficient system of free schools. They shall provide for the support of such schools by appropriating thereto the interest of the invested school-fund; the net proceeds of all forfeitures, confiscations, and fines accruing to this State under the laws thereof; and by general taxation on persons and property, or otherwise. They shall also provide for raising, in each township, by the authority of the people thereof, such a proportion of the amount required for the support of free schools therein as shall be prescribed by general laws.

SEC. 3. Provision may be made by law for the election and prescribing the powers, duties, and compensation of a general superintendent of free schools for the State, whose term of office shall be the same as that of the governor, and for a county superintendent for each county, and for the election in the several townships, by the voters thereof, of such officers, not specified in this constitution, as may be necessary to carry out the objects of this article, and for the organization, whenever it may be deemed expedient, of a State board of instruction.

Sec. 4. The legislature shall foster and encourage moral, intellectual, scientific, and agricultural improvement; they shall, whenever it may be practicable, make suitable provision for the blind, mute, and insane, and for the organization of such institutions of learning as the best interests of general education in the State may demand.

ARTICLE XI

MISCELLANEOUS

SECTION 1. No lottery shall be authorized by law; and the buying, selling, or transferring of tickets or chances in any lottery shall be prohibited.

SEC. 2. No charter of incorporation shall be granted to any church or religious denomination. Provision may be made by general laws for securing the title to church property, so that it shall be held and used for the purpose intended.

SEC. 3. The circuit courts shall have power, under such general regulations as may be prescribed by law, to grant divorces, change the names of persons, and direct the sales of estates belonging to infants and other persons under legal disabilities; but relief shall not be granted by special legislation in such cases.

SEC. 4. Laws may be passed regulating or prohibiting the sale of intoxicating liquor within the limits of this State.

SEC. 5. The legislature shall pass general laws whereby any number of persons associated for mining, manufacturing, insuring, or other purpose useful to the public, excepting banks of circulation and the construction of works of internal improvement, may become a corporation, on complying with the terms and conditions thereby prescribed; and no special act incorporating, or granting peculiar privileges to any joint-stock company or association, not having in view the issuing of bills to circulate as money or the construction of some work of internal improvement, shall be passed. No company or association authorized by this section shall issue bills to circulate as money. No charter of incorporation shall be granted under such general laws, unless the right be reserved to alter or amend such charter, at the pleasure of the legislature, to be declared by general laws. No act to incorporate any bank of circulation or internal-improvement company, or to confer additional privileges on the same, shall be passed, unless public notice of the intended application for such act be given under such regulations as shall be prescribed by law.

SEC. 6. For the election of Representatives to Congress, the State shall be divided into districts, corresponding in number with the Representatives to which it may be entitled; which district shall be formed of contiguous counties, and be compact. Each district shall contain, as nearly as may be, an equal federal number, to be determined according to the rule prescribed in the second section of the first article of the Constitution of the United States.

SEC. 7. [The children of slaves born within the limits of this State after the fourth day of July, eighteen hundred and sixty-three, shall be free; and all slaves within the said State who shall, at the time aforesaid, be under the age of ten years shall be free when they

arrive at the age of twenty-one years; and all slaves over ten and
under twenty-one years shall be free when they arrive at the age of
twenty-five years; and no slave shall be permitted to come into the
State for permanent residence therein.] [a]

Sec. 8. Such parts of the common law and of the laws of the State
of Virginia as are in force within the boundaries of the State of
West Virginia when this constitution goes into operation, and are
not repugnant thereto, shall be and continue the law of this State
until altered or repealed by the legislature. All offences against
the laws of Virginia heretofore committed within the boundaries
of this State shall be cognizable in the courts of this State in the
same manner they would be if hereafter committed within this State.
All civil and criminal suits and proceedings pending in the county
or circuit courts of the State of Virginia, held within the said
boundaries, shall be docketed and thereafter proceeded in before the
circuit court of the proper county; and all such suits and proceedings pending in the supreme and district courts of appeals of the
State of Virginia, if the defendant in the court below resides within
the said boundaries, or the subject of the suit is land or other property situated or being therein, and the plaintiff is entitled to prose-
cute in this State, shall be docketed, and thereafter proceeded in
before the supreme court of appeals thereof.

Sec. 9. The records, books, papers, seals, and other property and
appurtenances of the former circuit and county courts, within the
State of West Virginia, shall be transferred to, and remain in, the
care and custody of the circuit courts of the respective counties, to
which all process outstanding at the time this constitution goes
into operation shall be returned, and by which new process in suits
then pending, or previously determined, in the said former courts,
may be issued in proper cases. Copies and transcripts of the records
and proceedings of the said former courts shall be made and certified
by the courts having the care and custody of such records and
proceedings, or the proper officers thereof, and shall have the same
force and effect as if they had been heretofore properly made and
certified by the said former courts.

Article XII

Amendments

Section 1. No convention shall be called having authority to alter
the constitution of the State, unless it be in pursuance of a law
passed by the affirmative vote of a majority of the members elected
to each branch of the legislature, and providing that polls shall be
held throughout the State, on some day therein specified, which
shall not be less than three months after the passage of such law,
for the purpose of taking the sense of the voters on the question of
calling a convention. And such convention shall not be held unless
a majority of the votes cast at such polls be in favor of calling the

---

[a] The original form of section seven was as follows: "No slave shall be
brought, or free person of color be permitted to come, into this State for permanent residence." Congress made the adoption of the clause in brackets a
condition-precedent to admission into the Union.

same; nor shall members be elected to such convention, until at least one month after the result of the polls shall be duly ascertained, declared, and published. And all acts and ordinances of said convention shall be submitted to the voters of the State for ratification or rejection, and shall have no validity whatever until they are ratified, and in no event shall they, by any shift or device, be made to have any retrospective operation or effect.

SEC. 2. Any amendment to the constitution of the State may be proposed in either branch of the legislature; and if the same, being read on three several days in each branch, be agreed to on its third reading, by a majority of the members elected thereto, the proposed amendment, with the yeas and nays thereon, shall be entered on the journals, and referred to the legislature at the first session to be held after the next general election; and shall be published, at least three months before such election, in some newspaper in every county in which a newspaper is printed. And if the proposed amendment be agreed to during such session, by a majority of the members elected to each branch, it shall be the duty of the legislature to provide by law for submitting the same to the voters of the State, for ratification or rejection. And if a majority of the qualified voters, voting upon the question at the polls held pursuant to such law, ratify the proposed amendment, it shall be in force from the time of such ratification as part of the constitution of the State. If two or more amendments be submitted at the same time, the vote on the ratification or rejection shall be taken on each separately.

JOHN HALL, *President.*

ELLERY R. HALL, *Secretary.*

AMENDMENT TO THE CONSTITUTION OF 1861–1863

(Adopted in 1866)

ART. III. *Add to section* 1: No person who, since the first day of June, 1861, has given or shall give voluntary aid or assistance to the rebellion against the United States shall be a citizen of this State, or be allowed to vote at any election held therein, unless he has volunteered into the military or naval services of the United States, and has been or shall be honorably discharged therefrom.

SELECTED DOCUMENTS

The documents selected for this section have been chosen to reflect the interests or attitudes of the contemporary observer or writer. Documents relating specifically to the constitutional developments of West Virginia will be found in volume ten of <u>Sources and Documents of United States Constitutions</u>, a companion reference collection to the Columbia University volumes previously cited.

PROPOSED CONSTITUTIONAL CONVENTION

1871

The following statements concerning the proposed constitutional convention for West Virginia
just a few years after its formation indicates the issues involved and the views of various
groups and individuals.

Source: Granville Parker. The Formation of the State
of West Virginia. . . . Wellsburg, Va.: Glass and
Son, Book and Job Printers, 1875, 443-457.

THE PROPOSED CONSTITUTIONAL CONVENTION--
SHOULD IT BE CALLED--THE ADDRESS OF THE
STATE EXECUTIVE COMMITTEE OF THE DEMOCRAT-
IC PARTY TO THE PEOPLE.

Editors Pan-Handle News:

It was perhaps well enough for the last Legislature
to arrange to take the sense of the People on calling a
Convention, in accordance with one of the wise provisions
of our present Constitution, that permits no body of men
to take control of their Constitution without their ex-
press order and consent being first obtained. Though
after the Flick Amendment was passed and the disfranchised restored, there was no very obvious necessity
for the Legislature making such arrangement at present,
as the fitness of the present Constitution has as yet
been but partially tried and tested; and the admission
of the disfranchised upon their own solicitation into
the new Edifice, accepting it of course in the condition
they found it--furnished no ground. As well might a boy
or a dozen of them when arriving of age, or a company
of immigrants, or men relieved of Political Disabilities
through the Governor's pardon, claim as a right, to have
the People order a Convention to be convened and the
Constitution altered to suit their taste. That class of
the enfranchiesd that went to the Front in the late War,
and thereby established the sincerity of their profession
by staking their lives, so regard the matter, as the recent many and ingenuous statements of the Editor of the
Cabell County Press, fully attests. He was a brave
Confederate soldier, and is a Representative man among
that group who oppose the Convention as unnecessary at
this time, and laughs at the foolish hypocritical claims

of the Politicians now on their account, when the same
men either openly opposed the Flick Amendment, or ab-
sented themselves from the Polls; and among these the
Editors of the two Democratic papers which are now most
clamorous for a Convention, for the sake of these poor
Confederate soldiers who were necessarily absent they
say when the present Constitution was formed--but in
fact for the sake of the fat paying business as public
printers, they expect from the scheme if accomplished.
This class of the late Confederate soldiers that were
at the front, I honor and esteem, and if there really
existed any defects requiring a Convention to remedy,
and they should ask it--I would be among the first to
aid them, on the ground that our future interests and
and hopes were to be the same.

The only pertinent question now is: is it wise and
proper for the voter to order a Convention--and this
depends, I submit, on this further question: "Has
practical experiment so far, disclosed such defects,
otherwise irremidable, in our State Constitution, as
warrants the People to call a Convention to revise and
remodel it; and incur thereby the great expenditure of
time and money that will be required."

This is the question addressed to all the present
voters irrespective of antecedents, and no man who duly
appreciates its nature, magnitude and far reaching consequences that are to follow, will regard it as a partisan question, but one rising above all party consid-
erations.

The Address above referred to, has the appearance of
having been prepared with great study and care, inspired
by persons in the way of whose aspirations, and fossil
prejudices the present Constitution manifestly stands--
and hence among other aspersions, it is styled the "odious and unjust Constitution;" so this address can be
safely taken as stating all the defects and weaknesses
that can possibly be conjured up against the Instrument.
These I propose briefly to notice. I shall confine my-
self to those defects specifically charged, and pass
unnoticed the general denunciations and slang which any
blackguard can utter. I thought it a little singular
that the Executive Committee of one of the political
parties, should address the whole voters irrespective
of party, declaring it to be their conviction it should
not be regarded as a party question--and then in a few
sentences after, treat it purely as a party question,
and urge its party to turn out and vote for the Con-
vention--assigning as a reason, that the Republicans
in the Legislature voted against submitting the question
at all, and their press since had opposed the Convention.

How these statements can be reconciled with honesty and straightforwardness, I can't see--others may. But to their specific charges.

1st. They charge that since the people have put their party "partially" in possession of the Government, it is indispensable they should be put in possession of the whole; and a prime object of their Convention, I presume, is to rotate the present incumbents out. Their motives and feelings are patent, but how the public is to be benefitted by the operation, is not so clear; though they say "we owe it to ourselves as well as the whole people to see to it that we are not found wanting" in what? The natural inference is from what precedes in their address, it is in the devilment they have just been charging on their opponents. It would seem unnecessary for them to have proclaimed with so much emphasis their fixed determination in this respect. The people already anticipate as much, judging from their conduct last winter.

2nd. They charge in their indictment that the present Constitution was framed "amid the conflict of arms and throes of Revolution." This might have been the case where they were at the time, but there was nothing of it at Wheeling to disturb the deliberations of the Convention that framed the present Constitution. And still it must be acknowledged, there were eminent dangers and uncertainties hanging over the Nation at the time, that impressed its members with feelings akin to those felt when the Declaration of Independence was first proclaimed, and when our National Constitution was formed. Circumstances that cause men of whatever experience and capacity to have a lively sense of responsibility, and to act honestly and earnestly in whatever work engaged. Again, they say "those who framed it were few in number, representing but a small portion of our territory." This is untrue.

The number of delegates exceeded fifty, and all the Counties except Greenbrier, Monroe and Jefferson were represented. The able Editor of the Monroe County <u>Register</u>, a <u>Democratic</u> paper, who very likely was another Confederate soldier who went to the front--tells us in an article copied in the Wheeling <u>Intelligencer</u> of the 9th inst., how the people of his grand old County feel in relation to the necessity for calling a Convention. I wish I had room to quote it--'tis so much better than anything I can say. It may not be amiss to mention some of the present leading men of both political parties that were leading members of that Convention. The Hon. BENJ. H. SMITH, HON. DANIEL LAMB, HON. JOHN HALL. Would these men who now stand at the head of the Democratic

party of the State, make a Constitution that was "odious
and unjust?"

There were also, Hon. W. T. WILLEY, Hon. PETER G.
VAN WINKLE, Hon. JAMES H. BROWN, late President of the
Court of Appeals, Ex-Governor STEVENSON, Hon. LEWIS
RUFFNER; Circuit Court Judges, Hons. E. B. HALL, ROBERT
ERVINE, CHAPMAN J. STEWART, JOHN A. DILLE, THOMAS W.
HARRISON, the late E. H. CALDWELL; also Judge SOPER,
Hon. JOHN J. BROWN, Hon. JAMES W. PAXTON, the late Rev.
GORDON BATTELLE, Rev. JOSEPH S. POMEROY, Rev. T. H.
TRAINER and others equally earnest and patriotic, though
of less celebrity. Think these men, circumstanced as
they were, would have made a Constitution deserving to
be styled "odious and unjust!" And by whom? Let the
accusers answer, and reveal their own individual history during that trying period. But I return to the
indictment.

They further charge that after eight years experience,
portions of the Constitution have been "demonstrated
to be unsuited, very costly and unwieldy, and can be so
altered as to greatly simplify and save much money."
Where is the evidence of any such practical demonstra
tion? I aver, and am prepared to maintain, that the
Government when administered in accordance with the
letter and spirit of the present Constitution, is the
simplest and cheapest among the States of the Union.
The expensiveness heretofore, is wholly attributable
to vicious legislation, creating superfluous offices to
quarter partisans on, and to fraudulent and careless
management--none of which find countenance or warrant
in any part of our present Constitution. All which
abuses, the Legislature possesses the amplest power to
remedy; and when I voted the Democratic ticket last
fall, it was with the expectation a Democratic Legislature if elected, would at once remedy the monstrous
evils they had so long and so justly complained of.
Still they failed to do it to any considerable extent,
but started the scheme for a Convention, and the politi-
cian portion purposely retained this vicious legislation,
and sought to defeat the Flick Amendment and postpone
enfranchisement, so that by the combined use of the
two, they would get a Convention. The Flick Amendment,
thank God, they did not defeat, and now they are most
sedulously striving to foist this vicious legislation
upon the Constitution, and make the people believe it
grew there as its natural fruit. 'Tis a contemptible
scheme and worthy of its authors. The manifold abuses
hitherto, are no more the legitimate fruit of the present Constitution, than turkey buzzards are the legitimate fruit of the grand, sturdy oak on which they may

happen to perch.

Very Respectfully,

G. P.

June 16th, 1871.

THE PROPOSED CONSTITUTIONAL CONVENTION-- SHOULD IT BE CALLED--THE ADDRESS OF THE STATE EXECUTIVE COMMITTEE OF THE DEMOCRAT- IC PARTY TO THE PEOPLE.

<u>Editors Pan-Handle News</u>:

The question is: "Has practical experiment so far, disclosed such defects, otherwise irremidible. in our State Constitution as warrants the people to call a Convention to revise and remodel it; and incur thereby the great expenditure of time and money that will be required?" Commencing, then, where I left off in my last number:

3. Their next charge is: the great wrong for the people to refuse to call a Convention for the accommo- dation of the recently enfranchised. About this I have already said sufficient. The class that went to the Front have the good sense not to ask for it; while the other class, the skulking, cowardly politicans, who are the sole movers in this matter do not deserve to be gratified, unless they show good and sufficient cause exists outside of themselves.

4. Their next specific charge is, that Sec. 9, of Art. 4, of the present Constitution, confines the ap- portionments for choosing Delegates, that are to be made after each United States Census--to "white" popu- lation, omitting colored, who have since become citi- zns and voters. The editor of the Monroe <u>Register</u>, in the article before referred to, answers this so satis- factory, that I prefer to adopt his language in his reply to the Greenbrier County Editor, viz: "In reply we beg his attention to Art. I, Sec. 7, of the Consti- tution, viz: "Every citizen shall be entitled to equal representation in the Government; and in all apportion- ments of representation, equality in numbers of those entitled thereto, as far as practicable shall be pre- served."

"Under the Fourteenth Amendment accepted by West Vir- ginia, is not the negro a citizen, and under the Flick

Amendment recently adopted, does not our Constitution
make him a citizen? It is not necessary to be an opponent
of the Constitution, to settle that question."

The 9th Sec. of Art. 4, on which our contemporary rests
his position, must be construed as conflicting with the
now recognized "Supreme Law," and is therefore null and
void, as far as race is concerned.

This disposes of that count in their indictment. The
importance they attach to this count the reader may
judge by the way they close it, viz: "the bare statement
of this fact should be sufficient to convince the most
skeptical of the nexessity for a change in this regard."
What change could possibly give in this respect, what is
not already possessed through the Federal and our ore-
sent State Constitution, as already amended.

5.   Their next charge is, that the negro is not by
the Constitution chargeable with a poll tax; while the
"white" man is. Article 8, Section 2, of the Constitution which was formed before the negro was freed, provides that "white male inhabitants" of twenty-one years
of age shall pay a capitation tax of $1.00; but no where
forbids the Legislature imposing a like tax on the negro.
After the latter became free, in 1864, our Legislature
imposed a like tax on male negroes of twenty-one years
of age, and have continued to do so ever since, and the
negroes have paid without objection. See Code of West
Virginia, page 211, and session acts, 1864, page 16.
Having now become citizens and voters, to which under
our Institution, the obligation to pay taxes attaches,
it is just and right they should pay; and in their present status the Legislature has the unquestionable right
by the Constitution to impose the tax--being no where
prohibited in that Instrument from doing so; and if it
were otherwise, how easily the Constitution might be
amended in this respect by the mode the Flick Amendment
was accomplished, without any additional expenditure of
time or money--the Ratification taking place at the same
time the general election is held. But it is clear there
is no necessity for doing this even. If this imposition
of the tax on the negro, since 1864, has been unconsti-
tutional, why did not the last Legislature repeal the
law?

6.   Their next claim is, that the judiciary system
should be reformed "in toto," by which they mean, tore
out, and one of their liking put in the place. Their
animus for this is disclosed in the forepart of the address before referred to, where they say thay have put
"partial" possession of the Government, and the public
good imperatively requires they should have the whole.

All the present judicial officers from President of
Court of Appeals to Justices of the Peace, are to be
"reformed" or rotated out by their regenerated Constitution, and members of their Ring are to be rotated in.
Hence they are lavish and fierce in their denunciations
of this branch. They charge the present incumbents with
"weakness and inefficiency." They charge that their
decisions have been made from "partisan feelings and
favoritisms," and become "subjects of jibe and jest,"
that the Legislature has had to remove two of the judges.
They arraign the system itself as having failed to secure either "honesty, faithfulness, or capability," and
then complain because our Constitution gives to a bare
majority elected to the Legislature power, to remove
any judge for "misconduct, incompetence or neglect of
duty, or conviction of any infamous offence." But they
insist that the regenerated Constitution that is to
rotate themselves in, shall have high bars to keep themselves when once rotated in, from the "mere brute force
of the Legislature"--as they term it, requiring a majority of not less than two thirds of the Legislature
to reach them, however until they might prove or become.

Now this is about their view of this branch. Their
imputations upon the present incumbents are altogether
unmerited and unjust. And their suggestions of Reform
are irreconcilable and conflicting. They complain of
unfaithful Judges in one breath, and in the next breath
complain because our Constitution provides a speedy and
effectual way to get rid of such unfit and unworthy
Judges. Their suggestions are a senseless jumble, designed only to humbug the people, and rotate the present
incumbents out, and themselves in; and then put up high
bars to keep the people and their "brute Legislature"
at a distance! Our Judges are elected for terms of
six and twelve years, while our Legislators are elected
annually, and are of course more immediately responsible
to the people, their masters. This is why the people
intrust the Legislature with this corrective power over
the Courts. No faithful and upright Judge has cause to
fear, but one of the opposite character has cause to
fear. And, I submit, it is wise and right that the
people should retain this power over the Courts. Ab-
solve any men from responsibility for their actions,
and they become Tyrants. I here quote again, from the
editor of the Monroe Register: "Again regarding the reform of the Judiciary; the laws delay is the great com-
plaint. We are persuaded that the Bar has the corrective
entirely in its control. Moreover a speedy execution
of justice may be secured, by the institution of County
Judges of competent jurisdiction, holding monthly sessions." A specific amendment passed in the way the

Flick was, will insure this. But the Legislature possesses unlimited power to increase the number of Circuits and Circuit Judges, if found to be needed, without
any change in the present Constitution--power to make
each County a Circuit with a separate Circuit Judge,
if required.

7. Their next claim for a Convention is to adopt the
scheme of representation which secures to the minority
a certain amount of representation. The scheme is new
and untried; it has just been put on trial in some of
the States. It would hardly pay for our people to incur the cost of a Convention for the sake of embarking
in a mere experiment.

I again quote from our Monroe friend his remarks on the
township system and the ballot: "The Constitution only
provides six officers in each Township. A few of them
only receive nominal compensation. We consider the
Township system as the model of local self-government
and eminently American Democratic. Objection is made
to the ballot. We reply, God help the poor citizen
should its friendly shelter be torn from his homestead!
Does any sane man believe that any proprietor in the
Greenbrier Valley would hesitate to annihilate an unfor-
tunate dependant, who would dare to oppose his will by
a manly (!) viva voce, "No," at the Polls? Nobody in
Monroe believes that with a christian faith, we know.
It will not take twenty years as our contemporary says
to put fifty Amendments through the Legislature. Article 12, of the Constitution, places no restriction on
the number that may be proposed simultaneously." He re-
fers here of course to specific Amendments proposed by
the Legislature, and carried through as the Flick Amendment was.

This gentleman is not a resident of Wheeling, or
Charleston, but of an Eastern border County in the midst
of those "sparsely settled districts" where the Address
tells us the Township system is so unsuited and hateful.
Can we hesitate which party's testimony we ought to
take? And then, his estimate of the importance of the
ballot to every poor man in the State, compared with the
Old Virginian "viva voce." What honest heart does not
respond to the entire truth of what he says in this
respect. The politicans sigh for the return of the old
"viva voce," that enabled them to hold the poor and dependant, subject to their will, when exercising the
elective franchise. I have seen this purse power prac-
ticed in more States than one.

I have now answered I think all their specific charges,
upon which they declare our present Constitution to be

"odious and unjust," and ask for a Convention to remedy
it. There is no ground, I submit, for a Convention--
absolutely none; but only a necessity for the people
electing an honest Legislature and demanding that it
repeal all vicious, unnecessary laws, abolish all superfluous offices, and bring the Administration of the
Government to that simplicity and economy, which the
present Constitution contemplates, in all its departments, including the School system.

In my next I will endeavor to show the disastrous
consequences, and the vast expenditure of time and money, that must follow a sanction by the people of the
wild and wholly uncalled for scheme, of these politicians.

Very Respectfully,

G. P.

June 23, 1871.

THE PROPOSED CONSTITUTIONAL CONVENTION--
SHOULD IT BE CALLED--THE ADDRESS OF THE
STATE EXECUTIVE COMMITTEE OF THE DEMOCRAT-
IC PARTY TO THE PEOPLE.

Editors Pan Handle News:

As the people may not all of them be conversant with
Article 12, of our present Constitution, that provides
the two modes for amending the same, I will briefly ex-
plain them:

Section 1, provides that no Convention shall be called
for amending the same unless the people by a majority
of the votes cast at an election for the purpose, shall
order it; and if ordered, the delegates thereto shall
not be chosen earlier than a month at least after the
vote ordering, is officially declared. The final work
of the Convention is not to be valid until submitted
to the people and by them ratified.

Section 2, provides that the Legislature may at any
time by a majority thereof propose "any amendments to
the Constitution,: and such proposed amendments are to
be published in the papers throughout the State, three
months at least before the election of the succeeding
Legislature, which can approve or disapprove; and if the
former, it is its duty to submit the same at such time

as it shall deem best, to the people for ratification,
or rejection. If two or more such specific amendments
be submitted at the same time, the vote on the ratification or rejection shall be taken on each separately.
This last is the mode in which the Flick Amendment was
accomplished.

Now if the first mode is adopted by the people ordering
a Convention, they commit and surrender absolutely the
whole Constitution into the hands and absolute control
of such Convention, to do with it as it chooses, with
this single proviso, that the Convention shall submit
its "final work" to the people to be adopted as a whole,
or rejected as a whole, without the power of adopting
such parts as shall suit them, and rejecting the rest.
And hence the Legislature in its law last winter submitting the question, defines the powers and duties of
the Convention in this respect, if one be ordered, in
these words: "to consider, discuss, and propose a new
Constitution, or alterations and Amendments to the existing Constitution of the State." See Section 17, of that
Act; also Section 20, same Act: "The Convention shall
provide by ordinance or otherwise for submitting the
said Constitution" (meaning its "final work") "to the
people for ratification or rejection," as a whole of
course. The people of West Virginia certainly will not
put themselves in this disadvantageous condition in relation to their organic law, unless there is shown to
to exist some urgent, adequate necessity for doing it.
Have the politicians shown that necessity to exist?
But then, they tell us if we don't like the "final work"
of the Convention sufficiently to adopt it as a whole,
we can reject--which will leave the Constitution just
as it is now; they will have had a glorious jollifica-
tion and nobody will have been hurt. Ah! but who will
have to pay the cost of their grand farce? of course
we the tax-payers.

Whereas if the second mode be adopted, whenever particular amendments shall be shown by experience to be
wanted, any Legislature can propose any number of specific amendments, of these the subsequent Legislature,
having been chosen with reference to the pending proposed amendments, can approve or disapprove all, any,
or none, and in case any be approved, it becomes its
duty to submit such as are approved to the people at
the next general election, or earlier if the exigency
requires; when the people will have the right to adopt
or reject such as they choose; and incur no additional
expense whatever--and will all the while hold in their
own hands and exclusive control, their Constitution, instead of yielding it up as is now proposed, to the tender mercies of the politicians, to revel over, in a

gratification of their varied and in most cases, hostile
feelings. In any ordinary business matter, would any
prudent man hesitate which mode to adopt? The amending
of our Constitution when shown to require it, is purely
a practical business matter, of the highest importance.
But let us see for a moment what consequences must follow their proposed scheme if carried out. The Address
specially proposes to "reform" (which means change)
"in toto," the whole Judiciary system, and root out the
entire township which has now become so intimately in-
terwoven with our whole system of State polity. These
changes, if they should go no further, will necessitate
another new Code of laws--of the time and money required
for this, our people have had some experience of late.
I know the politicians tell us the mother State revised
her Constitution in 1829, and again in 1850, and in
neither case had a new Code made. I answer, neither of
these Conventions made Radical changes in the organic
structure of her State polity. They only modified to
some extent her basis of representation, and changed
the mode of appointing some of her officers. Her case,
therefore, is no guide to us, for our politicians propose to knock our present judiciary system and township
system out of the Constitution altogether; and all portions of the present Code that rest upon the parts removed, must of necessity fall and perish with them. A
new Code conforming to their regenerated Constitution
would become absolutely necessary to get ourselves out
of the legal chaos (so grateful to lawyers and politicians) which their scheme if allowed to progress, must
necessarily produce.

But the politicians as appears from their press and
talk, don't propose to stop where their address stops--
but propose abolishing the Free School system and the
ballot--restoring the old viva voce; also to remove
the present Constitutional restriction that prevents
the Legislature going into the same "log-rolling system"
that bankrupted the old State under the specious pre-
text of making "Internal Improvements." Behold the
old State with her forty-five millions of debt, and
then its product or result in her present internal improvements, which in fact never received but a small
portion of the money--the bulk having gone into the
pockets of her corrupt politicians. Look to the product
of this her vast expenditure, that remains within our
own Territory, and compare that product with what has
been done, and is doing, by individual capital and enterprise under the present policy of the New State; the
Chesapeake & Ohio Railroad for instance, which in a
year and a half will be completed throughout our State,
and connect the waters of the Chesapeake with the Ohio.
To accomplish which the old State had labored through

her politicians for forty years, and had accomplished--
what? But one thing is certain if our people after so
much labor and so much expenditure during the last ten
years in bringing our system of polity and Jurisprudence
to the point it is now in, and as now evidenced by our
new Code, containing the Constitution on which it is
based, now, or soon to be, in the hands of capitalists
and business men throughout the country--securing their
general approval and confidence as I have reason to be-
lieve--shall now idiotic like sanction the scheme proposed by the politicians, and go to work tearing everything up when there exists no cause whatever--we shall
forfeit the good opinion and confidence of that class
of men so essential to the future of the State. They
would as soon invest money in anarchial Paris, as in
West Virginia, while controlled by a people that should
act so insanely.

The politicians also complain that the present Constitution imposes too many restrictions on their powers;
that it is a "Code of laws," when it should be only "a
declaration of principles"--by which they mean--"glit-
tering generalities," that they may construe to mean
yes, or no, black or white, as may suit their corrupt
purposes. Now, if there exist defects in this respect,
it is because the present Constitution imposes too few,
instead of too many, of these safe-guards to our civil and
and religious rights.

Moreover, the "regenerated" Constitution they propose,
is to unseat every present holder of office in the
State. 'Tis impossible for them to confine their process of rotating out--(the prime object of their move)
to political opponents, but political friends, even
those elected last fall for two and four years, and as
yet hardly warm in their seats, must of necessity share
the same fate. Will these appreciate the necessity of
the politicians move? But the politicians are active
giving assurance throughout the State that they will
take care to save political friends. How save? Trust
them not. They have not the power to save, if they
would, when their ponderous rotating machine is once
set agoing. The only safety of such as are in exposed
positions, lies in preventing the starting of their machine, by turning out and voting down the Convention.
They have no safety in any other course. See and ponder
well the 17th and 20th sections of the law before quoted,
defining the powers and duties of the Convention, if
called.

One word now respecting the cost of their scheme should
it be accomplished, in which as a tax-payer I feel a
lively interest. Last winter as an auxiliary for getting

the Legislature to submit the question, a partian committee was appointed to report the probable cost of carrying through the scheme proposed not including the new Code, I presume; and this committee reported the total cost at $37,503--but omitted to give us the cents! The entire unreliability of estimates gotten up by politicians when they seek to get the Legislature and people committed to a favorite scheme, is felt and known to all. Those that have been made for building the Penitentiary, and completing the Insane Hospital, are fresh in the minds of all. The cost of advertising and printing and holding the required elections by the people, and the Convention, to cost only thirty-seven thousand five hundred and three dollars! Why the present Public Printers confidently expect to realize much more than that for their share of the spoils. And then add for the new Code a proportionate sum! Why only think, our present Code went into the mill in 1863, was constantly being elaborated in some form by well paid agents, and came out about two months since, requiring a period from seven to eight years, and costing over one hundred thousand dollars! And now the politicians modestly propose to knock both the Constitution and that in the head, and start de novo.

The official estimate made by GOV. STEVENSON last winter will not prove far out of the way. He certainly could not have had any personal motive to have overstated, and his large experience in such matters, his ample means for obtaining correct data, with his known care and accuracy of judgment--the personal and official responsibility on which he made the statement, entitle it in my judgment to the fullest credit. He estimated the total cost, reckoning both money and time (for business men reckon time as money) at about $350,000, 1-39 of which, or nine thousand dollars will be Brook County's share, which the tax-payers will have to pay-- and for what, let me in all earnestness ask my fellow voters and tax-payers? Suppose the township system was premature at the start in some of our sparsely settled districts (which I certainly not prepared to admit,) the system has become so interwoven with our entire State polity, including the Code, that it cannot now be torn out without lacerating and disemboweling the entire body politic, the restoration of which will require many years of persistent labor, and expenditure of vast sums of money. The genius of JEFFERSON originated the system in 1782, under the name of "wards," as embodying his ideal of a pure and perfect Democracy. Out of respect to his memory no true Democrat should too hastily cease his labor to realize that great man's ideal--especially when it is being so fully realized in all the great States on our North and West. Let us

then continue to advance in the direction we have
started. Let the Legislature abolish superfluous
offices, and repeal unnecessary, vicious laws, and
bring at once the administration of the Government to
harmonize with the simplicity and economy the present
Constitution contemplates; amend and improve our organic law as experience shall show it is required,
in the mode the Flick Amendment was carried through,
imitating more closely the organic laws by which the
old free States have attained to their present great-
ness--instead of turning back, as the politicians propose, and resuming for our young and vigorous State,
an obsolete organism fashioned in the interest of slavery, that is now abolished.

> "Let the dead past bury its dead,
> Act--act with the living present,
> Heart within, and God o'er head."

Mark one thing: if either political party commits
itself to the unnecessary, but purely selfish scheme
of these politicians, it will be sunk beyond hope of
recovery by its weight before it gets through with it;
and meantime, from its length of tail and many stings,
it will be painful to any party to handle.

> Very Respectfully,
>
> G. P.

June 30, 1871.

I afterwards published through the West Virginia
Journal of July 12, and the Wheeling *Intelligencer* of
August 5, 1871, what I hoped would satisfactorily answer
the specious claims for a Convention, made by Judge
FERGUSON, Col. B. H. SMITH and others, at a large meeting held at the Capital, and by the Hon. C. J. FAULKNER
at a like meeting at Martinsburg; but I was mistaken.
The Governor proclaimed the result of the election
the Fourth Thursday of August, 1871, to be 30,220 for
the call, and 27,638 against--2,582 majority in an aggregate vote of 57,858, and this after the colored
people and ex-rebels had been enfranchised, and were
free to vote.

Delegates subsequently chosen assembled in Convention
at the Capital the third Tuesday of January following,
formed and submitted for Ratification the fourth Thursday of August following, the present modified Constitution. During the canvass I submitted through the
Press the following remarks:

THE PROPOSED CONSTITUTION TO BE VOTED ON THE FOURTH THURSDAY IN AUGUST.

Editors Wheeling Intelligencer:

My self with other unprejudiced and unaspiring tax-payers opposed the calling of the Convention, for the reason we were unable to see any necessity for the expenditure of the time and money that would be required. A Convention, however, was called, as appeared by official proclamation, by a very small majority of those voting.

I have always regarded the making, or altering of a Constitution, in no sense a party question; and though political, as one of such transcendent importance, and the instrument of such permanent character--to shape in a greater or less degree the future organism of the State after we are in our graves and present political parties are extinct--as to imperatively demand of every honest citizen to lay aside all the little party prejudices, schemes and aspirations of the present hour, and approach the subject simply as a <u>citizen</u> and a <u>man,</u> who has the future welfare of his State, and posterity, as well as himself, to care for.

Entertaining these views I need not say with what regret, nay, disgust, I regarded the personal appeals to the most selfish passions of the voters that the Constitution make in order to induce an adoption of their work. . . . .

BLUEFIELD AND WEST VIRGINIA COAL

The following pamphlet illustrates the importance of southern
West Virginia, its coal fields,
other industries and the role
played by the city of Bluefield.

Source: <u>Bluefield, West Virginia</u>. <u>The Gateway to
Nature's Storehouse of Her Greatest Wealth</u>. N.P.

Bluefield is the foremost city of Southern West Virginia. It has grown and continues to grow faster than any city in West Virginia, and this growth is fostered by substantial business conditions which make for community prosperity. Situated midway between Cincinnati on the west, and Norfolk, Virginia, on the east, it has direct rail communication with the Ohio River city and the seacoast city, by the Norfolk and Western Railway, whose divisional headquarters and shops are located in Bluefield. Bluefield's growth, as shown by the census of 1910, was 142 per cent in ten years, and the indications now are that this increase will continue in an even greater ratio during the ten years intervening before the next census be taken. Bluefield's sky-line is taking on the aspects of a metropolitan city, Tall, modern fire-proof, and commodious office buildings, with floor space pre-empted in advance, are in course of construction, while still others are projected: new businesses are being established, while those already established are prospering, and the bank clearances of the city's prosperous financial institutions, increasing with each month, show, not only a steady increase in the volume of business being done in Bluefield, but prove most conclusively how substantial is the growth which the city is attaining.

COAL-FIELDS

There is a reason for Bluefield. It is the gateway to the Pocahontas coal-fields. Situated on the crest of the Alleghany Mountains, on the immediate east of these highly productive fields, it is not only the distributing point, both to and from the many mines and towns in the fields, but it is the "clearing house" for the coal product in a financial way. Many of the big coal companies maintain executive offices and sales agencies in Bluefield, and the business of mining and marketing the vast and ever

Bluefield, West Virginia

increasing tonnage of the big mines is conducted from the Bluefield offices.   The many large company stores scattered through
the coal-fields trade direct with the immense wholesale houses of
Bluefield, as likewise do the independent merchants whose stores
are legion throughout the length and breadth of the coal-pro-
ducing region.   The supply houses located in Bluefield also have
large demands made upon their complete stocks by the mines,
and the vast sum of money, into which the huge coal output of the
Virginia and West Virginia coal-fields is converted, finds its final
clearance through the Bluefield banks.

To secure a grasp of Bluefield's possibilities, one must naturally
have a complete conception of the immensity and magnitude
of the coal-fields contiguous and contributory to Bluefield, for
coal, after all, is the lifeblood of Bluefield.   The coal-fields—
that is the Pocahontas, the Clinch Valley, the Tug River and the
Thacker fields, all under active production, and which are com-
puted to have, at the lowest estimate, a two-hundred-year supply
of high-grade fuel under any probable scale of operation—cover
an area of approximately one hundred thousand square miles,
showing throughout the mountains a continuous seam of coal of
varying thicknesses.   There are four distinct varieties of coal,
as shown by the geological survey now on file at Morgantown,
West Virginia.   The Pocahontas is a particularly high-grade
coking and steam coal, bearing the reputation of being the best
steam coal in the world—a reputation which is evidenced by the
fact that it is the one coal which is selected by the United States
Government for use in producing steam for war vessels, and for
steam purposes in the construction of the Panama Canal. Dewey's
fleet moved to Manilla Bay under steam produced from Pocahontas
coal, when he destroyed the Spanish fleet in that memorable engagement, and Sampson's fleet was burning Pocahontas coal when
Cervera was so terribly licked at Santiago.

Along the Norfolk and Western, which, with its main line and
various divisions, penetrates to every portion of these fields, are
located Pocahontas and Tazewell, Virginia, and Bramwell, Welch,
Keystone and Williamson, West Virginia, all prosperous and
growing communities with large growing populations, and each,
being accessible to Bluefield by rail, is a feeder for the larger city.
By a branch line into Matoaka, West Virginia, the Norfolk and

Bluefield, West Virginia

Western taps the immense coal fields opened up by the Virginian Railway, and much of the trade of this prosperous section is thereby diverted to Bluefield.

NATURAL RESOURCES

Under the caption, "Natural Resources," as applied to the section in which is situated Bluefield, coal of course is the first consideration, but Bluefield has inherited from nature much more than coal. Limestone, of the very finest quality for cement purposes, abounds on all sides of Bluefield. Clay and shale, than which there is none better for brick making, is found in large quantities in and about the city, and there is within a ten miles radius of the city enough oak and poplar with which to keep a large furniture factory running continuously for years to come.

Not far distant from Bluefield, and on a down-hill haul all the way to the city, are rich deposits of iron ore, which when considered together with the limestone available hereabouts, and the cheap coal to be had in such abundance, makes a successful steel plant in Bluefield more than a possibility. This was noted by B. B. Burns, editor of the "Black Diamond," a coal trade journal, in an article which appeared from his pen as long ago as July 10th, 1910. He said:

"I found in the immediate vicinity of Bluefield some splendid deposits of limestone, and just to the south of it in Clinch Valley, served by one of the branches of the Norfolk and Western Railway, I saw evidences of an abundant deposit of iron ore. I was told by Dr. I. C. White, the State Geologist of West Virginia, that there was an abundance of iron ore in this territory, and I have before me a written statement of George H. Ashley, formerly of the United States Geological Survey, and now State Geologist of Tennessee, that there is an abundance of iron ore in the Cumberland Gap territory. Thus the Pocahontas coal coming down grade to Bluefield, and the limestone and iron ore coming up from the south, naturally meet and fuse at Bluefield, which promises to be the industrial capital of that section."

There is a mountain of silica in Bluefield from which may be obtained a magnificent glass sand, and this may be quarried at the top of the mountain, and after being ground can be brought

Bluefield, West Virginia

to the railroad level by gravity through a pipe line. Within the
corporate limits of the city, too. are great leads of yellow ochre,
known to be over fifty feet in depth. It has tested out as high-
grade, and has been passed upon as being especially adapted for
the manufacture of linoleums and high-grade paints. Not far
distant from Bluefield is a mountain of onyx of various colors and
surpassing beauty. Within the city proper there is likewise a
wide ledge of red and variegated marble which quarries readily
in immense blocks; there are also, within the city limits, out-
croppings of brown hematite iron ore, and fossil iron ore, and a
deposit of nickel as well. Just how extensive are the ledges of
these last mentioned minerals has not as yet been determined.
Bluefield possesses several mineral springs of high medicinal
values. There is a white sulphur spring, a yellow sulphur spring,
and a chalybeate spring, all of considerable volume and all
thoroughly impregnated with mineral properties. Taken by and
through the hills which surround the "Gate City," on all sides are
underlaid with a mineral wealth of an amazing variety and of
a value which, if realized upon, would rival the wealth of the
storied Aztecs.

CHEAP FUEL

Being in the heart of a coal-field most richly endowed by nature.
Bluefield possesses that for which so many cities strive—cheap
fuel. Expensive fuel necessarily retards the growth of cities.
while in every recorded instance. where cheap fuel is obtainable.
cities have sprung up and grown to large proportions, their
growth being directly attributable to the cheapness with which
fuel may be obtained. With coal mines at her door, giving forth
millions of tons of the very highest grade bituminous coal per
annum, Bluefield has coal for her manufactories and for domestic
purposes, at a cost of slightly more per ton than the drayage of
coal costs in cities remote from the producing centers. This means
much to the manufacturer already established in Bluefield, it
means much to the manufacturer in less favored sections seeking
better conditions—it means cheaper cost of production and an
increased power of meeting and overcoming competition.

HYDRO-ELECTRIC POWER

Bluefield is enabled to offer to the manufacturer and power user hydro-electric power at any required voltage, and at reasonable rates.

The Appalachian Power Company chartered and organized under the laws of Virginia, and managed by H. M. Byllesby & Company, has its general offices in Bluefield, and is domiciled in a handsome new office building devoted entirely to its uses. The Appalachian Power Company owns five separate power sites on New River, near Pulaski, Virginia, aggregating a total fall of 275 feet, or a total of 75,000 horse power. Two of these sites, numbers 2 and 4, have been completed, and together give a total of 29,000 horse power; work on the other three sites will be pushed forward rapidly to an early completion. The power from the sites already completed is being brought into Bluefield, over high-tension transmission lines, and these lines have been extended beyond Bluefield into the coal-fields, and many operations in the Pocahontas field are now being supplied with hydro-electric power.

Sub-stations have been constructed at Bluefield, and at Switchback, and Coalwood in the coal-fields, and through these sub-stations the current brought in over the high-tension lines is stepped down to a suitable voltage for distribution.

The cheapness of the Appalachian Power Company's hydro-electric power in Bluefield, and the contiguous territory, is not only increasing the output of the coal-fields, but is stimulating the growth of industries of all classes, in and near Bluefield. The Appalachian Power Company has a standard published scale of rates, and their guarantees insure to the investor and manufacturer a safe and economical power.

The Company is now constructing a second transmission line to this section, from their dams on New River, and will thereby be enabled to furnish additional power to meet the great demands therefor that the increasing developments require.

The management of the Appalachian Power Company, recognizing that the vast territory served by this power abounds in raw material; that it is centrally located, with a low freight rate, and enjoys cheap power, good labor and climatic conditions, has organized and equipped the first Industrial Department ever

Bluefield, West Virginia

organized by any power company. This department under the
direction of an experienced man, assisted by competent engineer-
ing, construction and power departments, offers to furnish, upon
application, rates, estimates and such information as is essential,
to prospective investors, manufacturers or industrial representatives who are seeking a location in this field, and will assist in
securing for them a location that will prove economical and
satisfactory.

SHIPPING FACILITIES

Bluefield enjoys exceptional transportation advantages. Being
the terminus of three divisions of the Norfolk and Western Railway, it is a pivotal point for shipments billed east or west, north
or south. Fast through freight schedules are maintained over all
these divisions, insuring quick service to and from the populous
centers, of the East and Middle West, and the manufacturer or
jobber located in Bluefield is in daily close touch with his custo-
mers. Freight rates have been equitably adjusted. There is no
discrimination by the railroad against Bluefield, and goods shipped
from or to Bluefield are handled by the railway company with
the utmost celerity and at a reasonable charge.

Bluefield, likewise, has excellent passenger train service to the
outside world, and while only a night's run from Cincinnati or
Columbus, or from Washington, Richmond or Norfolk, it is
slightly more than that to New York or to Chicago.

Distances from large cities to Bluefield are shown below:

	Miles	Hours
Roanoke	103	3
Lynchburg	157	5
Richmond	305	10
Norfolk	360	12
Washington	330	10
Baltimore	370	11
Philadelphia	465	14
New York	519	16
Cincinnati	327	11
Columbus	319	11

Bluefield, West Virginia

ELECTRIC CARS

Bluefield's street car system, controlled and operated by the Appalachian Power Company. is electrified, and is up-to-date, with frequent service between the business sections and surburban residences. There is also maintained a 20-minute service between Bluefield and Graham,· Virginia.

An electric road is projected through the coal-fields, and to Princeton, the county seat, 12 miles distant, and rights of ways have been surveyed for an extension of the electric lines converging at Bluefield to Tazewell, Virginia. and through the rich coal-field section to Welch. distant from Bluefield 50 miles.

MERCANTILE HOUSES

As a jobbing city. Bluefield takes first rank. It is the logical jobbing center of the coal-fields, and through its mercantile houses supplies the wants of more than half a million people. Her immense mercantile establishments are one of Bluefield's proudest boasts, and in themselves form a bulwark of strength for the future, indicating, as nothing else could, on how firm a foundation is the city builded. In Bluefield are four wholesale grocery houses whose annual trade will approximate two millions of dollars; a wholesale dry goods and notion house enjoying a business of a quarter of a million annually: a machinery and supply house, and a hardware establishment. which measure their annual sales by approximately one and one-half million dollars; a carriage and farmers' supply house. doing a splendid business; four produce and fruit jobbers, whose establishments have grown to large proportions; two large and a number of smaller lumber and supply houses, whose yearly shipments reach beyond the million-dollar mark; three distributing provision houses representing the leading Chicago meat packers; one jobbing house of musical instruments and musical supplies, and a furniture house second to none in the country.

RETAIL HOUSES

Bluefield. with its over a hundred retail stores, does the largest business of any city of its size in the country. Every kind of goods required by the city's trade is offered for sale. The

Bluefield, West Virginia

merchants are aggressive and progressive and are prompt in their efforts to present the latest styles and novelties of every kind. Bluefield attracts a volume of business from a fifty-mile radius that embraces a population of considerably over 200,000 prosperous people. The retail business in Bluefield has more than doubled in the last five years. In Bluefield is located one of the largest furniture stores south of the Ohio, and east of the Mississippi River; the store proper having a floor space of 49,000 square feet. Three drug stores are fitted throughout with the most modern and expensive fixtures, and two jewelry stores would be credits to Upper Broadway. Most of the clothing stores are equipped with the latest devices for displaying and the proper handling of their goods, and many of the grocery stores are at all times pleasingly decorated with the many delicacies for the table. Being only a night's run from Norfolk, sea-food is brought to Bluefield and served as fresh as in any seacoast city.

HOTELS

Bluefield is up to date in hotel accommodations. The Hotel Matz, which cost $250,000, is absolutely fire-proof, has a large lobby, seven dining-rooms, a banquet hall, a dance hall, a roof-garden, and one hundred and fifty bedrooms. It is equipped and furnished throughout with every modern convenience. The New Altamont Hotel, recently reconstructed and refurnished, has a large lobby, a spacious dining-room, and forty-four bedrooms. The Grand Hotel is up to date, with all modern conveniences and elegantly furnished. There are numerous smaller hotels and boarding houses in the city, and plans are being considered as this book goes to press for a hotel to be constructed on a scale of magnificence equal to those found in any city in the country. Bluefield's commercial importance is such that she entertains many visitors, and while already splendidly equipped for entertaining them, the demand for high-class accommodations is increasing, and provisions for meeting this demand will be made.

PAVED STREETS

All of Bluefield's business streets are paved with vitrified brick, substantially constructed on concrete foundation. In addition to the main streets, this paving was planned to take care of the

Bluefield, West Virginia

three principal approaches to the city; i. e., from Princeton, the county seat, on the east. Graham, Virginia, on the west, and Bland County on the south. These three thoroughfares are, likewise, now paved with vitrified brick and extended with macadam. Where the residence sections are reached the streets are parked with grass plots and trees on each side of the driveways, and are paved with tarvia.

Modern cement sidewalks have been constructed in all parts of the city, all brick sidewalks being replaced with cement, so that all the central part of the city is provided with this dry and easily cleaned walkway. The streets are cleaned regularly by the city forces, using sprinkling wagons and machine and hand sweepers.

DRAINAGE

Bluefield's drainage system has been installed on the pipe plan, all surface drainage carrying storm water, etc., being let into large pipes under the streets and carried off quickly; all house drainage being conducted into small pipes, where there is always plenty of water to carry away the sewage. These pipes lead to septic tanks, or sewage disposal plants, where the sewage is dissolved and filtered and the effluent carried off in the nearby stream.

BANKS

Perhaps there is no one thing that indicates the growth and development of a community more than a comparative statement of its banking institutions. Bluefield has just cause to feel proud of her banks, which have made a steady and satisfactory growth, as shown by the following summary of the four banks doing business here, two of which began business less than five years ago:

	Capital, Surplus and Profits	Individual Deposits	Resources
Oct. 1st, 1912	$771.159.96	$2.474,346.13	$3,560.509.09
Oct. 1st, 1911	714.000.00	2,050.000.00	3.123.000.00
Oct. 1st, 1910	677.000.00	1,623,000.00	2.605.000.00

CITY GOVERNMENT

Government by commission is the manner in which the city's business is conducted. The city's affairs are vested in four commissioners elected equally from the two political parties casting the highest number of votes in the city at the last preceding national election. The four commissioners transact the business subject to the veto power of a bi-partisan body of thirty-six councilmen from the nine wards of the city. The police and fire departments are organized and selected by civil service, and the selection of city officials is so arranged as to divide the government of the city equally between the two dominant political parties.

FIRE DEPARTMENT

With modern and well equipped central and suburban fire stations; fast and well trained fire teams, one of which is the fastest in the State; high water pressure of 120 pounds to the square inch; the Gamewell Fire Alarm Telegraph System, and the efficient men of the department, the citizens of Bluefield are reasonably secure from extensive and damaging conflagrations.

WATER

The water supply of Bluefield is furnished from never-failing mountain springs and is practically inexhaustible. Large steel reservoirs with concrete foundations are used for storage purposes, and all danger of contamination has been eliminated.

Bluefield, West Virginia

HE City of Bluefield has good schools, presided over by capable educators, and directed by a most efficient school board, who are ever alert to the welfare of the children whose education is entrusted to them. The new High School building, which cost over $130,000, ranks as one of the five best modern school buildings for the money expended to be found in the United States. In addition to class rooms, it contains a large auditorium, capable of seating twelve hundred pupils, equipped with a large and conveniently arranged stage; there is also a large, well lighted library and reading-room; offices for the Board of Education and administration officials; a magnificent gymnasium with running track, shower baths and locker rooms attached; a large store room; a rest room for sick and nervous pupils, with private toilet; principal's office; domestic science rooms; chemical, physical, and biological laboratories; a study hall sufficient to accommodate 200 pupils; an electric program clock; a telephone system; and a heating system combining the merits of direct steam heating with fan ventilation. This magnificent building is not only occupied by the High School, but by several of the grades as well. There are several handsome buildings devoted exclusively to the grade schools, located in various sections of the city, and another has just been contracted for.

Bluefield now employs fifty-six teachers; thirty-nine of these are employed in the grades, and seven in the High School. Music and drawing are taught by special teachers, and a skilled supervisor is in charge of the primary grades. The enrollment is above the 2,000 mark. Every effort possible is being put forth to make the course of study practical. The teaching force is as strong as that of any school of secondary grade in the State. Each department is in charge of a teacher especially trained for the work of that department, and all hold degrees from reputable institutions. Thoroughly equipped laboratories are in use for all

Bluefield, West Virginia

scientific subjects. The grade teachers hold Normal School diplomas or the equivalent, and are selected from a wide range of territory for especial fitness for the particular grade taught. At Athens, only eighteen miles distant from Bluefield, is located the State Normal Institute, housed in new, modern fire-proof buildings. and here the teachers of the State are perfected in their profession.

WEST VIRGINIA'S FOREST AND TIMBER INDUSTRIES

The following articles indicates
many aspects of the development
of the timber industries.

Source: A. B. Brooks, "The Story of the Forest and Timber
Industries," in James Morton Callahan. Semi Centennial History of West Virginia With Special Articles on Development and Resources. Published by
the Semi-Centennial Commission of West Virginia,
1913, 322-328.

The Story of the Forest and Timber Industries

By A. B. Brooks, Agent Plant Industry, U. S. Dept. of Agriculture.

There was a time not many years ago when nearly the whole land
area of what is now West Virginia was overspread with a forest of large
trees. On the cold mountain ridges and plateaus, in the deep river
gorges, and along the banks of the cool mountain streams were the cone-
bearing trees,—the hemlock, the pines, the balsam fir, and the red
spruce. With these, and covering thousands of acres of cove and hill
and river bottom, were the giant oaks and hickories and maples, and the
famous yellow poplar and the black walnut, intermingled with numerous
other broad-leaf trees, sought in after years for their valuable lumber
and fruits. These trees had grown and flourished and reached maturity,
like thousands of their ancestors, undisturbed and unused except by the
savage races and the wild animals that then lived in this otherwise un-
inhabited region.

When our forefathers came into this wilderness country and set themselves to the task of building homes and clearing the land for crops of
vegetables and grain, they found the forest a storehouse for many of
the necessities of life. While some of the trees had to be felled and
burned, others afforded indispensable materials for the construction of
dwellings and the manufacture of rude implements and tools. Thus it
was that the products of the forest first came to be utilized and that
forest industries were begun with the earliest settlements.

The story of the gradual but marvelous development of the various industries directly dependent upon the products of the forest can be traced
through the years in which farms have grown wide from the first small
openings and town and cities have sprung up throughout the state.

The remarkable evolution of the devices for the manufacture of lumber
is one of the best measures of the development of forest and timber industries. The adz and broad axe and frow, with which the puncheons
and boards were shaped for the first log houses, were the forerunners of
the whip saw and the old-fashioned water saw mill. The rude, hand-
operated device known as a whip saw was carried easily with other be-
longings of the pioneers and was used principally in the early days be-

fore heavy machinery could be brought in. The contrivance is thus described in Kercheval's History of the Valley of Virginia: "The whip saw was about the length of the common mill saw (referring to the saw used in water mills) with a handle at each end transversely fixed to it. The timber intended to be sawed was first squared with a broad axe, and then raised on a scaffold six or seven feet high. Two able-bodied men then took hold of the saw, one standing on top of the log and the other under it." The author of this history adds further on,—"The labor was excessively fatiguing, and about one hundred feet of plank or scantling was considered a good day's work for two hands." Straight-grained yellow poplars and white pines, and other trees with soft and durable wood, were easily found in those days and were always selected as whip saw material. Not a few old residences that were built of whip-sawed lumber are still standing. In Pocahontas county lumber was

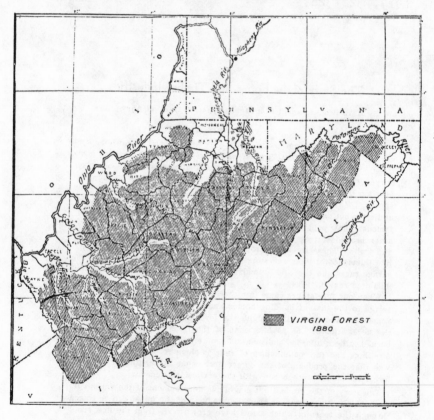

VIRGIN FOREST
1880

sawed with a whip saw for McClintic's Hunting House, built at the mouth of Tea Creek in 1880: and it is stated that saws of this kind have been used in Wyoming county, and in some of the adjoining counties of the southern part of the state, within the last ten years.

Whip sawing early gave place, in many sections, to the manufacture of lumber on water-power saw mills. Two types of mills belonging to this class were in existence. The sash saw mill consisted of a straight band of steel properly toothed, and strained taut by means of a frame, or

sash, into which it was fitted. The frame was pulled down by a water
wheel, which supplied the motive power, and was pulled back, in some
cases, by an elastic pole. The muley saw, introduced a little later, was
less cumbersome and was capable of more rapid work.

It is not definitely known when or where the first saw mill was built
and operated in West Virginia. It is probable, however, that there were
a few built by the early settlers who occupied the valley of the Potomac
river and its tributaries prior to the year 1755. No records have been
examined that confirm or deny this statement but it is reasonably safe
to say that there were a dozen rude water saw mills in the territory now
occupied by Jefferson, Berkeley, Morgan, Hampshire, Hardy, Grant, and
Pendleton counties as early as 1775, and that the number had increased
to five or six times as many by the year 1800. There may have been
more at each period. A record dated in the year 1810 states that there

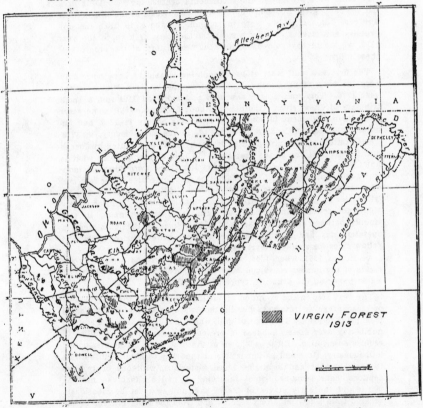

were about fifty saw mills running in Berkeley county alone at that time.

Those who left the settlements in the east to take up lands and
establish homes west of the Alleghanies had doubtless become familiar
with the water saw mill and knew its value, but many of them journeyed
such a distance that it was not possible for them to take anything so
cumbersome as machinery of this kind. As soon as the roads could be
cut through the wilderness, however, among the first things to be hauled
over them were the clumsy irons of these mills, which were taken farther
west, year after year, until they reached the Ohio river. The dates of

the settlements, therefore, nearly coincide with the dates of the beginning of the water saw mill industry. We find that there was a flourishing colony established on the Monongahela river as early as 1758; that there was a settlement containing five thousand people on the Ohio river near Wheeling in 1769; that colonies were established at Parkersburg in 1773, and at Point Pleasant in 1776. During the decade between 1770 and 1780 settlements were begun in a number of places along the Cheat river in Preston and Tucker counties; along the Tygarts Valley river in Randolph county; along the Monongahela and its West Fork and Tygarts Valley branches in the whole region now embraced by the counties of Monongalia, Marion, Taylor, Harrison, Barbour, Lewis and Upshur. During the same period, or slightly earlier in some cases, settlements were established on the Greenbrier river in Pocahontas and Greenbrier counties, and in the plateau and valley lands of Monroe county. Saw mills were brought to the settlements nearest the mountains first, but the dates given above are only a little in advance of the saw mills in any case. In fact, if we were to continue as above, to trace the progressive settlements step by step, from the very first up to the year 1880, we would have a reasonably accurate history of the progress of these mills.

The first saw mill west of the mountains is said to have been built near the town of St. George, in Tucker county by John Minear in the year 1776. This was a sash saw mill and stood on Mill run, a small tributary of Cheat river. Another was built by the McNeals some years after their settlement in southern Pocahontas county in 1765, and another by Valentine Cackley at Millpoint, in the same county, in 1778. The Gazetteer of Virginia and the District of Columbia, written by Joseph Martin, contains one of the first available lists of saw mills in what is now West Virginia. According to this list there were forty or more water mills running in 1835. Probably the most extensive water saw mill operations in the state were conducted on Middle Island creek and its tributaries in Pleasants, Tyler, and Doddridge counties. In Tyler county alone not fewer than twenty-four sash mills were running in this vicinity between the years 1840 and 1880. Some of the mills were in operation day and night in winter, and all sawed choice white and yellow pines for southern markets.

As late as 1863, when West Virginia had its birth as a state, seven-eights of the lumber consumed here and exported was manufactured by water power on the primitive types of saw mills.

The next step in the evolution of sawing devices was the introduction of steam-propelled rotary saw mills that were capable of being hauled from place to place. This type of mill, which is still in use in the state,—numbering over fifteen hundred in present operation—is too familiar to require description. Little is known of the first years of the steam saw mill industry. It would be impossible at this time to obtain full data as to their number and location. Local historians, with one or two exceptions, have remained silent regarding it, and all that can now be learned of the early stages of steam saw milling must be laboriously secured from a few imperfect records and from the older citizens of the state who were lumbermen many years ago. According to Martin's list there were fifteen steam saw mills in operation in the counties that now constitute West Virginia, in 1835. The increase in number of portable mills was not rapid during the first thirty or forty years after their introduction. With the coming of the railroads, however, mills of this kind began to multiply rapidly. New towns that grew up along these roads required a large amount of rough lumber for the hastily-built houses, and it was usually possible to locate mills near by. In 1870 J. H. Diss Bebar wrote: "Along both branches of the Baltimore & Ohio Railroad, from twenty to thirty first-class mills are cutting on an average 3,000 feet of lumber a day." And so it was along practically all other railroads as they were built from time to time. A few came at first and these were soon followed by many others, as mentioned in the quotation above. Just as the old water mills followed closely the first settlements, supplying lumber for floors and ceiling in the log houses and for the construction of the first frame dwellings, so the portable mills followed the later settlements as they were begun along the lines of the railroads.

The introduction of the band saw mill, about thirty years ago, practically revolutionized the lumber industry. The modern plant with its numerous mechanical appliances for the saving of labor and for rapid work, is a marvelous combination of ingeniously-fashioned machinery. The saw itself, as the name implies, is a belt of steel which works over two wheels mounted one above the other in a frame. The band is sometimes toothed on both edges so that a board is cut from the log at both the forward and backward movements of the carriage. The sawing, in the typical West Virginia plant, is usually conducted in the second story of the building. Logs, which are frequently conveyed long distances on trains and deposited in artificial ponds, are drawn up an incline to the mill floor by an endless chain device called the "bull chain." Here the log is scaled and deposited on an inclined platform sloping to the carriage onto which it is rolled and made fast by setting works, consisting of head blocks and dogs, operated by steam and controlled by levers manipulated by men on the carriage. The sawyer controls the movements of the carriage and handles the logs by the use of a device known as the "nigger" which plunges up from underneath and, striking the log with great force, tosses and turns it to any desired position. Slabs and boards are cut off in rapid succession, the carriage returning to the starting point at a high rate of speed. Mechanical carriers take the refuse and boards as they drop from the saw. The boards are conveyed to the edger saw and, without halting in their course, are carried to the trimmer, which, with its complicated system of levers and drop or lift saws, cuts off the uneven ends and reduces them to standard lengths. From here they are carried into the yard. The sound slabs are cut into proper lengths for lath or shingles or dimension stock, and the poor ones are ground into small pieces and passed with the saw dust into the furnaces. The time consumed in the passage of a log of average size from the pond to the yard and its conversion into lumber seldom exceeds three minutes.

Many of the large plants of the state are equipped with two or three band saws besides additional re-saws, and in some cases logs are squared and taken to gang saws where, with one passage, they are converted into boards. Several of the mills employ day and night shifts running twenty hours out of the twenty-four every working day in the year. The Richwood mill of the Cherry River Boom & Lumber Company—one of the largest operations in the state—cuts 300 thousand feet of lumber every day.

The first band saw mills were built in West Virginia between the years 1880 and 1885. Deveraux Lumber Company's mill built in Charleston in 1881 was probably the first. Two years later J. R. Huffman, the inventor of the band saw, built two large mills at Charleston. The St. Lawrence Boom & Manufacturing Company erected a band mill at Ronceverte in 1884; and the Blackwater Boom & Lumber Company erected one at Davis in 1887. Others of the older mills were those of the Hulings Lumber Company, at Hambleton; Gauley Lumber Company at Camden-on-Gauley; Parkersburg Mill Company, at Parkersburg; and Pardee & Curtin Lumber Company, at Grafton. There are at present eighty-three band saw mills in operation within the state.

During the years when the more primitive types of saw mills were running and continuing in some cases to the present time, were other forest industries of considerable importance. The list of these industries includes the making and floating of flat-boats, the rafting of logs and other timber products, the manufacture of cooperage stock, the hoop pole industry, shingle-making, the telephone and telegraph pole and cross-tie industries, tanning, and others of less importance. In later times the manufacture of pulp and paper has become one of the leading forest industries.

Rafting has been conducted on all the principal rivers of the state except those that are too rough to admit of it. On the Ohio river rafts of logs could be seen as early as 1830; and not far from the same time flat-boats were being made on the Kanawha, the Coal, and the Elk rivers. Most of the flat-boats were loaded with staves and taken to the salt works near Charleston where they were sold. For the past seventy-five years log rafts and single logs have been taken in large numbers from the forests that border the Guyandotte, the Big Sandy, the Little Kanawha, and other rivers. The hoop pole industry was enormous during the years of the early life of the state. As late as 1880, according to a report of the 10th census, more than three and three-fourths million hoop poles were cut, valued at $146,000. The hoop pole and shingle industries have declined within the past two decades. The cutting of poles and cross-ties, however, as well as the tanning industry, have steadily increased year by year, as the demand has become greater.

The amount of timber cut and used for various purposes prior to 1880 is not known. Much that was cut before the Civil War Period was used for domestic purposes. Some was sold in markets that could be reached by water and a little was shipped on the first railroads. One estimate puts the quantity used at home for buildings purposes, during the whole time before 1880, at 500 million feet. The cut of saw mills during the past thirty years has been about 20 billion feet. This does not take into account the vast quantity of timber cut for poles, cross-ties, tan-bark, pulp and for other minor purposes. The figures below show how rapidly the production has increased during the periods mentioned:

YEAR.	FEET BOARD MEASURE.
1880	180,120,000
1890	391,958,000
1900	778,051,000
1907	1,395,975,000
1909	1,472,942,000

West Virginia ranks first in the production of chestnut and cherry lumber, and thirteenth in the production of all kinds. The number of mills has been steadily increasing until at present there are fifteen hundred and twenty-four.

That the area of original forest in the state has decreased in proportion to the increase in capacity and number of saw mills is a natural and correct inference. The amount of lumber cut on the old water power mills and the amount rafted out, and that used for various other purposes, made only a small beginning on the margin of the great forests of the state. Even as late as the year 1880—as shown by the accompanying map—the great body of the coniferous and hardwood forests of the interior sections had scarcely been touched. At that date only strips of varying widths had been cut along the Ohio river and its larger tributaries in the state, and along the North and South Branches of the Potomac and Shenandoah rivers. But since the coming of the larger mills and building of additional railroads, the area of virgin forest has been reduced to less than one-tenth of its original size.

The forest and timber industries—beginning in a small way with the earliest settlements of the state, and increasing to their present large proportions—have meant more in the way of benefits to the citizens of West Virginia than any other industry except that of farming. All classes of people have been, and still continue to be, the beneficiaries of these forest industries; and only by being deprived of the advantages that come from this source, as is so frequently the case, will the people come to realize their great dependence upon the things that reach them through this channel.

The forest industries have not only brought capital into the state and afforded employment to thousands of its citizens, but have also been the means of establishing social centers and developing wholesome social customs. Hundreds of small villages and flourishing larger towns of today stand where lumber camps formerly stood, built long ago in dense wooded regions. In these camps a rough but large-hearted, robust, and justice-loving company of young lumbermen—some from the rural homes of the state and others from outside our borders—constituted the first temporary and shifting population of these centers,—a few lingering behind as the first permanent residents. In many instances, where the ownership of large tracts of timber land has fallen into the hands of a single company, the first small operations have soon given place to enormous mills which still furnish employment to the entire population of the prosperous towns that have grown up around them.

WEST VIRGINIA'S RAILROADS

The following article indicates
various aspects of the development of the railroads during
West Virginia's first half
century

Source: Hon. Henry G. Davis. "The Railroads in the
Development of West Virginia," in James Morton
Callahan. Semi Centennial History of West Virginia
With Special Articles on Development and Resources.
Published by the Semi-Centennial Commission of West
Virginia, 1913, 305-309.

That the railroad is a necessary factor in the development, and the
most important agency in the commercial expansion of a state, is an
admitted truism, and it is particularly emphasized in the history of West
Virginia. This state stands pre-eminently at the head of all the states in
the Union, not only as a priority, but also as to the physical strength,
financial standing and commercial importance it has attained through
this agency.

West Virginia, a hill state seemingly impassable, unexplored and
sparsely settled, with a determination to engage in the commerce of the
country, was a pioneer state in inviting a project of railroad building,
when it joined hands with Maryland in assisting the construction of
the first railroad in the New World. It has continued to co-operate with
railroads in proposed construction, and as a consequence ranks high
as one of the most important commercial states in the Union in every
line of industry and agriculture.

The first method of communication between West Virginia and the
eastern coast was by means of the old National Pike which ran between, Baltimore, Cumberland, Md., Uniontown, Pa., and Wheeling, W.
Va. Baltimore at that time—between 1805 and 1852—was the eastern
market for West Virginia and Ohio, and commerce was conducted by
mean of long trains of Conestoga wagons, for which the rates of service
were high.

Wheeling, by means of its geographical location on the Ohio River,
was the principal river town west of the Alleghenies and one of the
leading centers of trade of the vast country now comprising the Central
West. Its greatest business however was confined to the river traffic
between Pittsburg, Cincinnati, Louisville and St. Louis.

In 1827 the Legislature of Maryland passed an act to incorporate
a joint stock company, styled the Baltimore & Ohio Railroad Company,
the building of which was begun on July 4th, 1828, with the Ohio river
as an objective point.

West Virginia soil was first reached at Harper's Ferry on December
1st, 1834. The great struggle of crossing the almost impassable mountains began at that point; and in 1836 the city of Wheeling was officially
considered the most suitable western terminal from a commercial point
of view, and surveys were completed through this portion of Virginia.

The State of Virginia (the commonwealth of Virginia was not sepa-
rated into two states until June 20th, 1863), subscribed to the building of
the line through the state, as did also the city of Wheeling, and it was

determined to hurry the completion of the through line by building east-
ward from Wheeling to meet the line coming west. This line was practically completed to Fairmont in 1852, its progress being slow because
all materials had to be hauled from eastern mills through unbroken
mountains.

On December 24, 1852, the two lines were officially united at Roseby
Rock, West Virginia, and the first through train from Baltimore to
Wheeling left the Maryland city on January 10, 1853.

The wedding of the Ohio River with the Chesapeake Bay was the occasion of a great celebration, for it meant to Northern and Western
Virginia the dawn of a new era in business. It placed the territory in
direct communication with the markets of the country, and the superior
transportation facilities over wagon methods encouraged the investment of
capital in the development of West Virginia industrially.

The railroads in sixty years covered 3556 miles, growing at the approximate rate of 60 miles a year.

While these figures are startling, another feature should be considered
at the same time; when these railroads were built, the money came
into the state from points outside the state; the railroad property being in the state became assessable to the state for taxes, showing a double
profit to the state. It should further be considered that the railroads
naturally gave employment to the people in the state.

From the Auditor's report of the taxable property of railroads in the
State of West Virginia for 1912, the total amount paid to the state on
such property was $1,401,092.32.

As a matter of record, the following list of steam railroads in West Virginia
with the mileage and assessed value of each, is appended:

		Miles of main track in State	Assessed Value
1.	Alexander & Eastern Railway Co.	14.50	$ 25,000
2.	Buffalo Creek & Gauley Railroad Co.	19.00	100,000
3.	Benwood & Wheeling Connecting Railway Co.		60,000
4.	Belington & Northern Railroad Co.	4.06	30,000
5.	Baltimore & Ohio Railroad Co. System	1,071.61	77,650,000
6.	Big Sandy & Cumberland Railroad	.30	2,000
7.	Beaver Creek Railroad Co.	6.25	15,000
8.	Cranberry Railroad Co.	12.00	50,000
9.	Cairo & Kanawha Railway Co.	15.91	60,600
10.	Campbell's Creek Railroad Co.	13.33	135,000
11.	Cumberland Valley & Martinsburg Railroad Co.	24.48	500,000
12.	Cumberland & Pennsylvania Railroad Co.	.21	18,000
13.	Coal & Coke Railway Co.	196.75	4,900,000
14.	Chesapeake & Ohio Railway Co. System	641.52	35,000,000
15.	Dry Fork Railroad Co.	29.86	500,000
16.	Erbdon & Summersville Railroad Co.	6.00	20,000
17.	Elk & Little Kanawha Railroad Co.	21.00	250,000
18.	Glady & Alpena Railroad Co.	18.00	80,000
19.	Guyan, Big Ugly & Coal River Railway Co.	10.00	40,000
20.	Glenray & Richwood Railroad Co.	9.00	40,000
21.	Hampshire & Southern Railroad Co.	38.60	425,000
22.	Iron Mountain & Greenbrier Railroad Co.	26.59	50,000
23.	Island Creek Railroad Co.	6.77	375,000
24.	Kanawha & West Virginia Railroad Co.	37.38	550,000
25.	Kanawha & Eastern Railroad Co.	.75	3,000
26.	Kanawha Central Railroad Co.	4.70	30,000
27.	Kellys Creek & Northwestern Railroad Co.	6.35	60,000
28.	Kanawha, Glen Jean & Eastern Railroad Co.	14.20	300,000
29.	Kanawha & Coal River Railroad Co.	12.00	50,000
30.	Kellys Creek Improvement Co.	6.16	36,000
31.	Kanawha & Michigan Railroad Co.	99.44	1,750,000
32.	Lorama Railroad Co.	14.00	55,000
33.	Longdale Iron Co. (Mann's Creek R. R.)	9.00	16,050
34.	Little Kanawha Railroad Co.	30.44	200,000
35.	Lewisburg & Ronceverte Railway Co.	5.75	37,550
36.	Loop & Lookout Railroad Co.	5.00	35,000
37.	Meadvale & Somerville Railroad Co.	11.00	20,000
38.	Morgantown & Kingwood Railroad Co.	48.74	1,000,000
39.	Marlinton & Camden Railroad Co.	10.50	78,000
40.	Norfolk & Western Railway Co. System	437.77	32,500,000
41.	Pickens & Hackers Valley Railroad Co.	16.50	45,000
42.	Pickens & Addison Railway Co.	19.00	45,000
43.	Panther Railroad Co.	7.00	5,000
44.	Pittsburg, Wheeling & Kentucky Railroad Co.	28.02	2,000,000
45.	Pittsburg, Cincinnati, Chicago & St. Louis Rwy. Co.	29.30	1,368,695
46.	Preston Railroad Co.	14.00	30,000
47.	Pocahontas Railroad Co.	7.00	20,000
48.	Piney River & Paint Creek Railroad Co.	6.36	125,000
49.	Randolph & Pocahontas Railroad Co.	19.00	100,000
50.	Raleigh & Pocahontas Railroad Co.	1.25	100,000
51.	Sewell Valley Railroad Co.	21.00	125,000

DOCUMENTS

109

52.	Stroud's Creek & Muddlety Railroad Co.	6.00	80,000
53.	Valley River Railroad Co.	11.00	45,000
54.	Virginian Railway Co.	139.60	5,500,000
55.	Wabash-Pittsburg Terminal Railway Co.	4.85	550,000
56.	West Virginia Midland Railroad Co.	42.06	140,000
57.	West Virginia & Southern Railroad Co.	3.10	40,000
58.	West Virginia Northern Railroad Co.	10.97	110,000
59.	Winifrede Railroad Co.	7.43	150,000
60.	Wheeling Terminal Railway Co.	7.28	800,000
61.	Western Maryland Railway Co.	197.65	10,000,000
62.	Walkerville & Ireland Railroad Co.	6.25	15,000
63.	White Oak Railway Co.	10.44	225,000
64.	Winding Gulf R. R. Co.	......	2,500
	TOTAL	3,556.98	$181,666,795

Another fact to be considered is that railroads are compelled to lay out such an enormous amount of money in building, that it takes years to begin getting anything like a reasonable return on the money, as compared with any other business. It is not generally known but it in a fact nevertheless, that every railroad in West Virginia, fifty miles or more in length, with probably one exception, has been in the hands of receivers at sometime.

Whether or not such receivership was occasioned through the extravagant expenditure of the railroad's money, the state has been benefitted by this expenditure.

The first commodity that West Virginia had to offer to the country was its bituminous coal, and to make this of any value, railroads were built into the coal fields to get it to the market. The coal being of a desirable quality, the market demand was great. In the year 1912 there were 65,000,000 tons of coal shipped out of the state and at the average price of $1.00 per ton at the mine, the state became $65,000,000 richer.

Just what influence and effect railways have upon values is illustrated in the following table of comparison of property values of certain counties in West Virginia, all of which were without railways in 1880; since which time railways were built in two of them:

COUNTIES WITHOUT RAILWAYS	Property Values 1880	Property Values 1912	Total Increase	Per Cent.
Hardy	$2,428,122	$5,267,456	$2,839,334	116
Pendleton	1,587,953	4,420,715	2,832,762	177
	4,016,075	9,688,171	5,672,096	141
COUNTIES WITH RAILWAYS				
Randolph	1,102,474	22,497,425	21,394,951	1,940
Tucker	479,702	13,688,517	13,208,815	2,753
	1,582,176	36,185,942	34,603,766	2,187

The assessed value of railways alone in the latter two counties in 1912, was as follows:

Randolph $4,770,632

Tucker 2,510,737

While the percentages of increase in Randolph and Tucker counties, which have only a few miles of railways, over the percentages of increase for Hardy and Pendleton counties that have no railways, is enormous, the proportion of increase in other counties that have more railways is even greater.

Railroads bring not only wealth, but also enlightenment and convenience to the communities through which they run. Compare for instance the hardships, inconvenience and loss of time when traveling by stage coach, with the cheapness, comfort, and dispatch of the modern train.

A very small percentage of the traveling public ever stops to make a comparison between the swiftly running train of today and the stage coach of not so many years ago. Just think what it would mean to the business man of this generation if he had to go from New York to San Francisco in a prairie schooner to keep a business engagement. Today a man may conclude his business in Chicago, leave in the afternoon, comfortably settle himself in a palatial train and be in New York, a thousand miles away, for business in the morning. And think of the comforts he may enjoy enroute. Meals served in attractive dining cars; the use of a well stocked library; barbershop; bath; stock market reports; stenographer; valet service and nearly all the comforts of a hotel.

Notwithstanding all this, the cost of the trip is far less than it could have been made for in the stage coach days. Such a journey could not have been made with a team in fewer than twenty five days at a cost many times in excess of the present day service afforded by railroads.

And yet there are those who delight in anathematizing these great common carriers without which we would not have our present day development and progress.

Apropos of the way in which the railroads annihilate distance, it may be interesting to the reader to insert here a time table of 1835-36, for the winter arrangement of a stage line well known in those days:

"The Mail Pilot Line leaves Columbus for Wheeling, daily at six a. m., reaching Zanesville at one p. m., and Wheeling at six a. m. the next morning.

"The Good Intent Line leaves Columbus for Wheeling, daily at six p. m. through in twenty hours to Wheeling (127 miles) in time for stages for Baltimore and Philadelphia."

But, let us take a simpler example of the great benefit of the railroads. Let us suppose that a farmer wished to visit a point sixty miles away. Before the days of railroads it would have required at least three days to go and come, and transact his business while there. He would have had to supply himself with nine meals; his team with the same, count the wear and tear, to say nothing of losing the use of his team on the farm or figuring his own time.

How different now! He boards a train after breakfast, reaches his destination in an hour and a half, transacts his business and is home again for supper in the evening—all at the cost of a trifle as compared with the old way.

Surely the people are indebted to the railroads, and West Virginians are no exception.

Considering these facts showing what the railroads have been to West Virginia in the past sixty years, how much more important they must be for the state's future under the present tremendous business activity.

West Virginia as a mineral and agricultural state has recently proved its claim that it affords more opportunities in these directions than any other state; and bids fair to become one of the leading fruit producing states in the Union.

The manufacturing possibilities of the state with its cheap fuel—coal and gas—are beyond computation. Therefore it stands to reason that new railroads will have to be built, and as has already been pointed out, the cost of building and maintaining a railroad in such mountainous country as West Virginia, is infinitely more than in a level country, it will require a large investment of capital. However, where the construction of new lines is warranted by the laws of supply and demand, the capital will be forthcoming. Just so long as the railroads prosper, so will the state prosper, and the reverse of this statement is equally true.

MEDICINE AND PUBLIC HEALTH

This article indicates the
development of medicine and
public health facilities
up to the beginning of the
second decade of the 20th
Century.

Source: Dr. Charles A. Wingerter, "Development of Medical Practice and Public Health," in James Morton Callahan. Semi Centennial History of West Virginia With Special Articles on Development and Resources. Published by the Semi-Centennial Commission of West Virginia, 1913, 538-551.

The task put before the historian is the presentation of the thing as it was. It is the function of history to present to an on-looker the outward thing, and to show the reader as much as a spectator would have seen, illuminated by a knowledge of the past and a judgment drawn from succeeding events. A picture of the conditions of medical practice and of public health in West Virginia at the beginning of our half-century of existence as a state, would be the best background upon which to mark the notes of advance and change. To outline this vision, we could perhaps do no better than to put ourselves in the place of one of the old-time physicians in one of the central towns of the region at the period just before the war. Let us suppose him established in his practice and then ask ourselves what was the character of his preparation for his work; what the extent of his knowledge and equipment; what the character of his clientele; what his relations to them and to his fellow physicians; what co-operation, if any, the public authorities offered to him in his labors; what were the details of his daily life and practice, and what the rewards and remunerations of his work.

To the spectator of his person and life this follower of the healing art will appear in no wise extraordinary, nor will his uneventful years seem to demand attention different from that given to the life and work of any one of his fellow-citizens. Nevertheless, this ruddy old gentleman, somewhat stern of countenance, somewhat shabby of attire, somewhat brusque and forbidding of manner, is a man of rare human greatness, a man who is leaving his indelible mark upon the neighborhood as he drives the country roads in his ceaseless rounds, night and day, summer and winter. He is to the manor born; here among these common hills he first saw the light of day; the people to whom he ministers are the boys and girls with whom his boyhood days were passed. To them he is "Doctor John" or "Doctor Will." He knows their secret sorrows as well as their open joys. With sealed lips, with busy hands, with generous heart, he fits into every home in the very remotest of the mountain districts. The foot-falls of his horse have sounded upon every highway and by-path and tortuous trail leading to a human habitation, no matter how forlorn or neglected it be, no matter how degraded or destitute the dwellers therein. He means more to his generation than words can tell. He means much to them at that dread time when "pestilence walketh abroad," and when the ears of the stricken listen eagerly for the doctor's coming, knowing that he will not fail them in their evil hour. But he means no less to them after the shadow of the pestilence is lifted, and the every day life is resumed.

When the common miracle of human birth is awaited, and the doctor is
groping his weary way through the darkness of the night to serve as a
comfort and a help to an anguished mother; when the wailing cries of
the helpless infant have called him, and the fretful child is surrendered
fearlessly to the soothing mercy of his rugged but tender arms; when by
his mere presence he renews hope in the breast of the father and mother
whose growing child lies sick unto death; when the feebleness of declining
years lays the parent low, and the anxious helpmate and the weeping children hang upon the lips of the doctor in their eagerness to learn if they
may further hope; when he sits by the bedside, to smooth the pillow and
hold the hand of his childhood friend in the dying hour; in all these
emergencies the presence and sympathy and counsel of our old-time doctor
are sources of strength and comfort.

The half-century that marks the life of the young state of West Virginia
witnessed the passing away of this old-time physician, whose welcome face,
with the iron lines of struggle in mouth and chin, and the softened lines
of humor about the deep-set eyes, was wont to haunt the quiet inland hills
and glades and valleys. To the thoughtful reader his passing away must
needs be accompanied by a nameless, aching sense of irreparable loss.

Simple was his preparation for his work. First of all, before he could
think of taking up the study of medicine, he had to be touched by the
divine fire of love for his fellow men. Cupidity uttered no call to him.
The doctors whom he saw and knew were never anything but poor in this
world's goods. Not one of all their number left a competency for his
family, and more than one died in dependence and poverty, if not in absolute want.

As was the custom of the time, a custom gone out of vogue gradually
during the half century we are chronicling, our young altruist and
aspirant for the profession became a student under one of the practitioners of his acquaintance in the neighborhood. His time of apprenticeship would extend through a period of years varying from three to seven,
dependent on circumstances that were variant in each individual case.
During this period the young student would have the advice and direction
and example of his preceptor. He would have access to the doctor's scanty
library; but the beginner's knowledge of medicine was acquired not so
much from reading and study as from association with the doctor. He
rode with his preceptor on his rounds, held the basin when the patient
was bled, and helped to adjust plasters, bandages and splints. In the office
he ground the powders, mixed the pills, made the tinctures and infusions,
washed the bottles, served as office-boy, and in addition performed the
most menial duties. In this method of teaching the personal element was
so pronounced that everything, in fact, depended upon the preceptor, save
what natural talent and industry might accomplish.

The self-reliance, the readiness, the expertness and the knowledge of
human nature thus acquired, went far to compensate for the lack of
more modern methods of preparing for the actual work of medical practice. Anatomy could be studied only by observation of the living body
and by the aids of the doctor's books and plates. Dissection was out of
the question, unless the student was one of those fortunate few who
could supplement their years of apprenticeship by one or two terms, of
four months each, at some medical college in a neighboring state.

Once entered into practice, armed with all the advantages for the ac-
quirement of knowledge that the time afforded, the doctor of this period
was yet poorly equipped, if he were to be judged by our modern standards.
Modern physiology, the splendid structure built upon the scientific foundations laid in the first half of the nineteenth century by Johannes Mueller
and Claude Bernard, was then unknown. Humoral pathology, based
on the discarded theory that all diseases are due to the disordered
conditions of the humors and fluids of the body, was the only guide to the

doctor in the formation of a judgment concerning the malady that afflicted his patient. Rudolph Virchow, the father of the modern cellular pathology that has shed such a brilliant light upon the processes of disease in the human organism, was then teaching and writing. He published the results of his first important studies in 1850, but the ready acceptance of his views had to await the new era that was not yet fully dawned. Medical chemistry, as we know it today, unlocking the secrets of the body fluids in health and diseases, had not yet been developed.

The microscope had been known to mankind for centuries. but its modern use in clinical medicine was as yet unforecasted. Pasteur had already, in the late fifties, made his first illuminating discoveries in bacterial chemistry, but not till the seventies was the knowledge of virulent microbic diseases attained.

Laennec gave the stethoscope to the world in 1819, but for a generation it was looked upon as a medical toy. The treatises upon the practice of medicine used in the colleges to which our prospective practitioner would have gone, gave no inkling of the importance to mankind of this instrument of diagnosis.

Other instruments of precision that aid in the making of accurate diagnoses, instruments that are in constant use by the physician of today, were unappreciated by the old-time doctor in our state. The ophthalmoscope had been given to the world by Helmholtz in 1851, and the laryngoscope by Czermak in 1858, and the common forms of the various specula were being devised; but they were not in the instrumentarium of the general practitioner. The first sphygmograph was not imported to America until 1870. In that same year the usefulness of the hypodermic syringe and of the fever thermometer was urged upon the doctors of the state. They were informed that a good syringe could be obtained for four dollars, and a pocket-sized fever thermometer at a cost of three dollars and a half.

The materia medica of the period was consistent with the old humoral pathology then in vogue. One of the leaders of the profession in our state, who belonged to the new era but was conversant with the old. tells us that his predecessors "believed that the patient was nothing if not bilious; and believed that there was practically but one organ in the body, the liver, and that this was to be unlocked at stated intervals, and entered and swept and garnished with mercury; and believed, moreover, that in at least half of the known diseases, salivation and salivation were synonymous terms." Another medical writer, referring to early therapeutics in our state, confirms this, saying: "Calomel was the sheet anchor. In the way of medicine, all other remedies were considered subordinate to this, and its use was usually pushed to salivation." And still another, writing in 1879, makes this statement: "Not many years ago Calomel was considered the indispensable drug in practice. Our predecessors, without calomel, were artillerymen without ammunition—Sampsons shorn of their locks. The tongues that were swollen, the teeth that were loosened, the gums that were made tender, will present a horrible array of testimony when doctors get their deserts." Happily there were other remedies in the doctor's saddle-bags.

Fevers of various kinds called for treatment. Along the Ohio river, where the population was densest, intermittent fever was common. It was rare in the tier of counties immediately back of the river, and was almost unknown in the central area. It was treated with the bark of dog-wood, cherry and poplar digested in whiskey, or with a decoction of boneset. Remittent or bilious fever was the summer and fall disease, and on its incursion the patient was generally vomited freely with lobelia, after which he was purged with infusion of white walnut bark, and sweated with copious draughts of warm elder-blossom tea. The value of powdered cinchona bark for malarial disease was known, but the amount required to restore the patient was so great, and the supply so small, that the remedy was all but useless. Quinine, the alkaloid of the bark, was unknown until 1820, and, though obtainable, was still very costly in the late sixties. One of the most dreaded diseases was dysentery. It was treated by the internal use of "oak-ooze," May-apple root and walnut bark, slippery-elm bark tea, and bitter elm bark, regarded as a specific; hot fomentations were applied to the abdomen.

"Lung-fever" was a blanket-term to cover many obscure inflammations of the chest. Without the stethoscope it was difficult to diagnosticate in a clear and definite manner the ailments now known to us as pneumonia, bronchitis, pleuro-pneumonia, pleuritis, empyema, hydro-thorax, and incipient phthisis. Heart troubles such as pericarditis, endocarditis, and hydro-pericardium, with their attendant disturbance of respiration, made the problem more complex. The diagnosis of "inflammation of the chest" once having been made, however, the patient was steamed with the vapor of whiskey or hot water, and in addition drinks made from herbs were given him and herb-poultices were applied externally. Virginia snake-root was considered a remedy for coughs of all kinds. Rheumatism, which was common then as now, was treated with cohosh, blood root and the bark of leather-wood, and sometimes the patient was given an "Indian sweat." Cupping was the usual external remedy for rheumatic pain as well as for neuralgia, and was freely prescribed. Blood-letting, or "depletion," fell into disuse on the eve of the new era. In its day, however, the lancet was called into use for the most diverse ills. If a person was severely injured he was bled at once; when a damsel fainted a vein was opened. Indiscriminate blood-letting; excessive purgation; mercurialization; starvation; leeching and blistering; all these are mile posts of the past. Such was the armory of the olden practitioner. The mere recital adds graphic touches to the picture of his daily life and practice.

Disease and death, the attendant scourges of humanity, did not relax their hold in favor of the mountains and valleys of western Virginia. About twice in a decade the old doctor was called upon to fight epidemics of measles and of scarlet fever. For neither of these did he have an adequate remedy, and in his experience, as in ours, the scarlet fever proved often fatal. There was no inhabited locality of the State that was entirely free from typhoid fever. It is recorded that the Asiatic Cholera was existent in this region in the fifties, and it is known to have recurred in 1864. In 1857, a noteworthy endemic of diphtheria made its appearance. Many of the more experienced practitioners were of the opinion that they had treated sporadic cases of this form of sore throat many years before under the name of "putrid sore-throat." Be this as it may, there can be no doubt that in 1857 the disease was well-marked and frequent, and often affected whole families with singular fatality. The modern boon of the diphtheria antitoxin was not among the weapons of the doctor of the late fifties, and, because of that fact, he was obliged to stand with heart devoid of hope at many a bedside.

For lack of statistics, it is impossible to tell the exact number of "doctors" practicing in the counties of the present state at the time of its formation. A careful student estimated that West Virginia contained in 1877 "612 physicians and surgeons." In this enumeration it was calculated that there were from 376 to 400 regular physicians. the remaining 236 being eclectics, homeopathists, Thompsonians, herb doctors, or cancer doctors. It is surely fair to presume that fifteen years earlier, the number of physicians in the vast extent of the state was considerably less. It would doubtless be more than a generous estimate that would place at 200 the number of regular practitioners in 1862. Concerning the character of their attainments a friendly contemporary writes: "In West Virginia the profession is, at many points, adorned by one or more active, intelligent members, who, by their industry and devotion to science, have

made for themselves a name outside of their fields of labor; and there are
others, too, of modest talent, scattered here and there, who but require
the contact of association which a proper organization would so surely affect, to develop latent powers and capabilities of great credit to themselves, individually, and beneficial, in the highest degree, to their patients
and the commonwealth of medicine."

When the doctor's saddle-bag, "with its horn balances and its china
mortar," was the only drug store within half a hundred miles, other
sources of therapeutic aid than his often had to be drawn upon in times
of emergency. Then was the hour of the bustling house-wife, or of the
crooning dame in the chimney corner. The treasures of domestic medical
lore, not unmixed with much alloy of superstition, were then brought
forth and sagely estimated. Or the old-fashioned family almanac was
taken down from its nail by the window. Following this, the embryo
botanists of the household were despatched to ransack the native flora of
the neighboring hills and dales for suitable materia medica. If per-
chance it were the season when mother earth was barren, then recourse
was had to the household cupboard, or to the shelves of the village store,
where were to be found simple drugs, stowed away among the heaps of
shoes, Rohan hats, balls of twine, packages of seeds and flitches of bacon.

In the intervals between these urgent periods of stress and storm when
sickness had entered the lowly doorway of the country home, a primitive
prophylaxis, of the domestic brand, served to keep alive, in the minds of
the good folk, the thought of "the ills to which flesh is heir." More medicine was then taken every year by the well than is now taken by the sick.
Remedies now in the medicine-box of every farmer were then utterly
unknown, but in their stead medicines now quite gone out of fashion, or
at most but rarely used, were taken in generous quantities. "Each spring
the blood had to be purified, the bowels must be purged, the kidneys must
be stimulated, the bile must be removed, and large doses of senna and
manna, and loathsome concoctions of rhubarb and molasses were taken
daily."

The men and women to whom ministered the doctor of half a century
ago were, taken by and large, a single-minded, simple-hearted folk, and
the mutual relations of the profession and the people were cordial and
sincere and, on the whole, satisfactory to both. While the reward and
remuneration to the doctor were of little account in the pecuniary sense,
while

> "Little gold had he gathered, little gear had he won,
> His wealth but the mem'ry of noble deeds done,"

there was added recompense, notwithstanding, in the love and reverence
which his patients accorded to him, and in the naive awe with which they
regarded his calling, shedding a glamor about it that was not all unde-
served. Warm tears of gratitude for life preserved and health restored
made some amend for sleepless nights spent in anxious watchings over the
sick. The modest and loyal doctor was not without his heart-burnings,
however. Human nature is ever the same, and here, into these mountains and glens, as elsewhere and in every age, the impudent and pre-
suming charlatan found his way, and, by his pleasing address and se-
ductive suggestion, often weaned away from truth and science the devotion of the unsophisticated.

Between the lines of the foregoing sketch of the old-time doctor and
his patients, the reader will discern the ready evidences of the spirit of
individualism that pervaded the community in all matters that related
to the health of the inhabitants. It was the evening twilight of an age
dominated by individualism. "Each one for himself" was the thought in
the various members of the community. A day and time were soon to
dawn when a different spirit would prevail; when the thought that
would tend to find a place, unconsciously at least, in the minds of men
would be "One for all, and all for one." This was to have its effect in

drawing together the interests, private as well as public, of the dwellers in what is now West Virginia. Before the war, however, each individual householder, in the country districts especially, was a solitary unit of sanitary administration, concerned alone in the safeguarding of himself and family.

From the modern viewpoint, the negligence of the state in matters of health was simply appalling. The statement might be made in strictest truth that absolutely nothing was done by the public authorities of the commonwealth to preserve the health of the people. Even as late as 1878 the only legal regulations that could be deemed sanitary in character were few and totally inadequate, and, such as they were, they proved futile because of want of proper enforcement. Of course, any trade or occupation proven injurious to health might be enjoined or removed as a nuisance. When a mill-dam was condemned, inquiry was to be made whether the health of the neighborhood would be endangered by the stagnation of the water or otherwise. There were also on the statute books provisions against the selling of unsound or adulterated food, drink or medicines. These laws, however, were dead letters. An enactment was made in 1861 providing that the Governor appoint three persons to act as vaccine agents. located in Wheeling, Charleston and Martinsburg, who were to collect and supply vaccine matter to any citizen who might apply for it. Each one of these agents, appointed annually, was to receive as remuneration for his services twenty-five dollars a year. In cases of destitution. local overseers of the poor were allowed to furnish free vaccine matter and to provide for vaccination at the expense of the township.

Previous to 1881 there was absolutely no enactment on the statute books of the state regulating the practice of medicine. The regular practitioner had no legal status whatever. Whenever the terms "physician" or "surgeon" were mentioned in the laws, as for instance in the provisions concerning inquests, examination of lunatics, appointments to the Colonel's staff. to the hospital for the insane, to the penitentiary, and the like, they applied without distinction to the intelligent and scientific physician and to the murderous pretender and quack.

Thus were the people neglected by the state in the important matter of their health and physical well-being. The individual citizen had to depend, for the preservation of health, upon his own care and efforts, aided and guided by the devotion and advice of the lone family doctor. When that strength and resource failed, the destructive processes were left to triumph.

Consultation by two or more physicians at the bedside of the sick. so common to-day, was then rarely possible. The means of inter-communication were difficult, tedious and expensive, and the nearest neighboring physicians were not only far distant, but were often strangers to one another. Each one pursued in dreary professional isolation the daily routine of his practice, storing up such clinical facts as may have fallen under his observation, relying on his own strength and wisdom and. courage as he silently wrestled with the tremendous problems of life and. death. This isolation of the doctor is to be noted as one of the salient marks of the profession at that time. The physicians of western Virginia were as well equipped in character and attainments and ideals as were those of like numbers in any part of the country in the early sixties. The individual units of the guild were worthy factors of social service, but there was absolutely no cohesion in the mass. Without proper understanding of one another, most often without acquaintance even, scattered far apart, the only bond of union that held them was the catholic love of their fellowmen and the common inspiration of their noble calling.

Such was medical practice in the present West Virginia on the eve of the new state's birth. To grasp fully the import of the changes that

followed, the reader must bear in mind that there were at work two great forces—the one world-wide, silent and constructive; the other national, clamorous and shattering. The light of a new era of medical science was abroad in Europe and its rays had reached to the present confines of the Mountain state. The scientific world was just awakening from the long sleep of the eighteenth century. The science of medicine was stirring uneasily in token of an early rousing. Here in the loyal counties of the Old Dominion, however. the premonition of the destined conflict at arms numbed the energies of the profession of medicine as it did all other civic activities. Over the whole state brooded that terrible quietude, that oppression of the union between quietude and terror, that was felt as in a dream from which one might awake screaming. It was like a thin cord stretched tight, that might snap with a noise like thunder.

The terrible stillness was broken at last by the bugle note of war. The lethargic souls of men were roused, and thousands of immortal spirits were soon blazing with alternate hope and fear. The sword had been drawn; and the sword is "a magic wand—a fairy wand of great fear, stronger than those who use it—often frightful, often wicked to use. But whatever is touched with it is never again wholly common. Whatever is touched with it takes a magic from outside the world." War had come to put an end to an evil peace, and that old thing—fighting—made men young again, and it brought to the medical profession of West Virginia as new a birth as came to the state itself.

Most obvious and superficial of the results of the medical participation in the great conflict was the rise of surgery to a distinct accomplishment. The fiery and bloody ordeal of the war gave an impetus to American surgery that quickened into activity the entire surgical world, and the profession of our own state had its full share in this triumphant rejuvenescence. In 1863 it was still optional at the University of Pennsylvania for the student to take the course in operative surgery, and it was limited to amputations and ligation of arteries. Lister had not yet begun his studies on the causative relation of germs to pus formation in wounds. Suppuration, secondary hemorrhage, septicemia, pyemia and "hospital gangrene" were frequent and dreaded complications of operation, and "surgical fever" was its usual accompaniment. A wounded joint generally involved the loss of the limb. Compound fractures and dislocations gave cause for serious alarm. The preparation of a patient for surgical treatment meant rest, tonics, purgation and selected diet. For purposes of disinfection about the place of operation solutions of chlorinated soda and of nitrate of lead were used. Castile soap and water were employed for cleansing at the site of incision. Frequent recourse was had to strong escharotics, chief among them being nitric acid, Condy's solution of permanganate of potash, a solution of bromine, or the actual cautery. Prepared lint and charpie were used for dressings. With inefficient resources the surgical practice of fifty years ago had to contend against formidable difficulties. The success that it achieved was largely due to the personal qualities of the surgeon himself. "And there were giants in those days." The camp and field of war developed many operators, skilled, expeditious and masterful. The marvellous development of military surgery on the battle-grounds gave an impulsion to the surgical art that extended into civil life after the close of the war. Amputation, ligation of arteries, excision of external tumors. lithotomy by the perineal route and surgical treatment of stricture make up the list of the chief operations that afforded opportunity in civil practice for the skill and daring of the old-time surgeon.

Less obvious than the development of surgery, there was another result of the war that was vastly more significant and far-reaching in its effects upon the medical profession. This was the recognition of the

duty and value of unity of action. All men's eyes had been raised to
see the vision of national union. The loyal hearts in the state were fired
with ardor to maintain it; and the same flame that kindled the patriotism
of the soldier likewise melted away the barriers of the individualism that
encompassed the citizen. A new spirit was born of the war—the spirit of
co-operation. Men learned that combination is stronger than witchcraft,
and that it brought to them something from outside themselves, something
positive and divine, something that mere disjoined individuals can never
possess. The energy of this new spirit touched the medical profession
and, uniting with the newly enlightened medical science that had already
come from over the seas, ushered in the New Era of Medicine in West
Virginia.

The new leaven of the spirit of union, cast into the old elements of the
profession already existing in the state, soon transformed the whole mass.
The modern conceptions of medical science took on vigorous life, and the
old ideals of the profession took on reality. Not invention, but renovation.
was the note that marked the new era. Medicine awoke and began working, not upon. but in. its material. Heretofore each worthy member of
the medical profession had felt himself held by an invisible bond to all
other worthy fellow-workers. The hour was come for them all to be united
into a visible brotherhood, to be brought face to face, to touch shoulders
and to clasp hands. The ideal was to be stiffened with reality.
In a very few years an organization was accomplished that gathered
together at its annual meetings the best members of the profession from
all the most distant parts of the state, from the Kanawha on one side, to
the waters of the Shenandoah on the other; from the Panhandle in the
North, to the Greenbrier region in the South. In February, 1867, a call was
issued for a convention to be held in April of the same year at Fairmont,
for the purpose of organizing a State Medical Society that would eventually take in "all members of the regular profession." Twenty-one physicians answered roll-call at the Fairmont meeting, which adjourned to
meet at Wheeling in October, 1867, in semi-annual session. At the end of
the Wheeling meeting sixty-two members were enrolled, and when the
society met at Clarksburg in 1869 the roster contained almost 100 names.
As far back as 1835, and again in 1847, tentative organization of the
local medical profession had been accomplished in Ohio county. The
records now extant of these early organizations are too scant for further
survey. In August, 1868, however, a new organization, the Ohio County
Medical Society, was effected, and it has continued in vigorous existence
till this day. Mason, Wood, Cabell, Lewis and other counties caught the
same spirit of union, and at an early period of the new era were sending
delegates to the annual sessions of the State Medical Society. In this
jubilee year these and many other local associations of medical men are
flourishing throughout the state. Very early in its existence, the "Medical
Society of the State of West Virginia" caught the vision that pictured the
state busying herself in protecting and fostering the public health. The
transactions of the early meetings record discussions on public sanitation
and hygiene; on the history, causes and prevention of epidemics, and on
other like topics. An evident appreciation was shown of the great
truths that disease is an enemy not only to one, but to all, and that prevention is better than cure. The project to promote the creation in West
Virginia of a modern state board of health soon found adherents in the
organized profession, and definite steps were taken towards realization.
Much work of an educational character had to be done, however, before
any part of the project could be realized.
In the winter of 1875 an effort was made to procure an act of the
state legislature that would establish a State Board of Health. This

venture failed. A second effort was made in 1877, with the added impetus afforded by a recommendation of the governor, favoring the act, in his message to the legislature. The project met a second defeat, however. One of the members of the legislative body who opposed the bill said on the floor of the House that his opposition was based on the belief that "No one would get sick or die until his time comes." The physician who, as a member of the legislature, had moved the passage of the health act and had strenuously urged its enactment, reported its failure to the meeting of the state medical society. He added, however, that he felt, upon reflection, that he had shown more zeal than sense in urging it, since the question had never been agitated in the state, and the people in general knew little or nothing about "state medicine." He concluded with saying, "It is our first duty to get this subject rightly before the people, and to have them understand that they do not get sick and die until there has been some violation of some physical law, or until their three score years and ten are passed." Then began the active propaganda on the part of the profession, having for objects the instruction of the populace concerning the true meaning and scope of sanitary laws and their administration, and the awakening of a living faith in their importance and efficiency. That campaign has been waged with varying fortunes ever since, contending against the prejudice of the legislator, the defiance of the venal journalist, the arrogance of the charlatan, and the ignorance of "the man in the street."

The first real promise of ultimate success in this warfare for the health of the people came with the passage by the legislature on March 8, 1881, of "An Act to establish a state board of health, and regulating the practice of medicine and surgery." This act went into effect in June following, and provided for the appointment by the governor of two physicians from each congressional district, who were to be "graduates of respectable medical colleges, of not less than twelve years continuous practice, and distinguished by devotion to the study of medicine and the allied sciences." The persons so appointed constituted the state board of health; their term of office was for two years. The secretary was the executive officer of the board and it was his duty to correspond with local boards of health, to give needful advice, to visit on request localities where endemics, epidemics, infectious and contagious diseases, or other unusual sickness were prevalent, and to adopt proper regulations for their suppression. The board as a whole was to take cognizance of the life and health of the inhabitants of the state, and cause to be made sanitary investigations, and inquiries concerning the causes, prevention and methods of remedying diseases in men and domestic animals; to advise with regard to the location, drainage, water supply, heating and ventilation of coal mines, and the drainage and sewerage of towns and cities. It was given power to establish and maintain quarantine when invasion of the state by infectious or contagious disease was threatened. The Act further provided for the establishment of county boards of health. These, and such local boards as were already established in cities and towns, were to be auxiliary to the state board of health, and to act in harmony with it.

The practice of medicine was regulated by provision of the Act that required the possession of a certificate from the board by any person professing publicly to be a physician, prescribing for the sick or appending to his name the letters "M. D." The certificate was obtained in the following manner. If the applicant were a graduate of a medical college recognized as reputable by the board, it was sufficient for him to present his diploma for verification, as to its genuineness, to those members of the state board of health appointed for his congressional district. If he were not a graduate of such a medical college he was required to pass a satisfactory examination before the two members of the state board in his district, together with the presiding officer of the local board of health of the county in which the examination was held. Physicians who had been en-

gaged in the continuous practice of medicine in the state for more than
ten years prior to the passage of the act were given a certificate on the
presentation of an affidavit as to the number of years they had been in
practice. Itinerant physicians were permitted to practice on paying to
the state board of health a special tax of fifty dollars for each and every
month, and fraction thereof, during the period of their practice. The sum
of one thousand dollars was appropriated from the state treasury to pay
the salary of the secretary of the board, and the travelling and other necessary expenses incurred by the members in the performance of official
duty. No other compensation was allowed them. Moreover, the board
was required to pay into the state treasury all money received for certi-
ficates, or collected from fines and special taxes. As will be seen from a
study of this digest of the first health law of the state, the newly created
board of health was merely an examining and advisory body. It was
given no power nor means to do real constructive work in the interests
of the public health. With its establishment, however, the first mile-
stone had been planted on the road to better things.

During the winter of 1881-1882, by the establishment and rigid enforcement of quarantine against the cities of Pittsburg and Alleghany, the new
health board saved West Virginia from the ravages of small-pox. The
appropriation from the public treasury proving inadequate, the doctors
of the state made up a private fund of several hundred dollars to insure
energetic administration of the law in this emergency. The early and
concrete proof of the wisdom of the new health law appealed to the
thoughtful, and, as a result, during the adjourned session of the legislature, in 1882, there was a demand for the establishment of a permanent
health law. The governor declared in his message to the legislators that
"the preservation of the public health should be one of the first concerns
of the government," and he strongly urged sufficient appropriation. Accordingly, "the Amended Act of 1882" was passed in March. In several
particulars the amended act was an improvement upon the law of the
previous year. It carried an unconditional appropriation of fifteen hundred dollars per annum for the support of the State Board of Health; it
provided for payment out of the county treasuries for service rendered
and expense incurred by local boards; it stipulated that, though a county
court might nominate the local health board, the State Board should have
the right to confirm or reject nominations; it granted to local boards
ample powers to enforce local quarantine; and it required "itinerant
physicians" to pay the monthly tax in every county in which they prac-
ticed.

"Chapter 150 of the Code, concerning the Public Health," substantially
as enacted in 1882. has continued until this year to mark the limit of ad-
cance made by the state in the matter of safe-guarding the public health.
Minor changes were made in its provisions in 1895, 1901 and 1907. The
time of continuous practice required for eligibility to membership on the
board was reduced first to ten years and later to six. The term of office
was lengthened to four years, and a per diem of four dollars allowed for
time of actual service. Changes were made in the details of examination
methods. The dawning of West Virginia's semi-centennial year. thus
found the state board of health no more than an examining and advisory
board, except in times of threatened epidemic. The fees from the applicants for license to practice repaid the state treasury for the expenses of
the board. In other words, the potentiality of the body to promote the
health of the people by positive and constructive measures was still
curtailed by lack of adequate powers, and the cost of its maintenance was
borne by the medical profession.

The legislature of 1913 signalized the jubilee year by making important
amendments to the Public Health Law. These provide that the secretary
of the board, to be named by the governor. shall be ex-officio State Health

Commissioner, devoting his whole time to the duties of his office, and possessed of the powers pertaining to offices of like kind. He is allowed a salary not to exceed three thousand dollars per year, with travelling, clerical and other necessary expenses incurred in the performance of his official duties within the state. The board is given power to maintain a laboratory, and to employ such chemists, bacteriologists, servants and agents as are needful for the proper performance of its functions. These provisions are made efficient by an appropriation of fifteen thousand dollars annually for the uses of the board. Two additional features in this advanced health legislation of 1913 are worthy of note here. One makes it the duty of all county or municipal officers to meet with the State Board of Health, or its representatives, at least once a year to attend a school of instruction for the purpose of becoming familiar with their duties in the interest of public health. The other directs the State Board to provide vaccine lymph, diphtheria antitoxin, tetanus antitoxin or any other serum preventives of disease, free of charge to the poor and indigent, and in other cases where in its judgment it may be necessary to prevent contagion. Already in 1911 the legislature had passed an act providing for the establishment and maintenance of a tuberculosis sanitarium under the supervision of the state board of control. Terra Alta in the glade country was selected for the site, and the institution is now a reality. This move forward in the crusade against tuberculosis was confirmed by the legislature of 1913, which also appropriated funds to be used in educating the people concerning the means of preventing and eradicating "the great white plague."

West Virginia has made an infinite stride forward in state medicine during the fifty years of its existence. The half-century began with no provision for the public health; it closes with a splendid health law on the statute books of the state. The first general hospital in what is now West Virginia was founded at Wheeling in 1850. It was the only chartered institution of the kind in existence here at the inception of the new commonwealth. Within the last score of years, however, hospitals have been established in all parts of the state. Some of the smaller communities, even, can now boast of hospital service; and a system of Miners' Hospitals inaugurated by the state in 1899 is giving excellent results in a restricted field of effort. To many of these hospitals are attached training schools for nurses, each sending out annually its quota of young women skilled in the art of ministering to the sick and wounded.

Medical practice in West Virginia has gone forward steadily during the last five decades, keeping pace with the advance of the science and art of medicine throughout the nation. The physicians of the state can be reckoned in thousands, and their character and attainments are of a high order. The profession at large has been elevating its standard by encouraging among its members a strict adherence to the high ethical code that is set to guide them. The State Board of Health has aided in the attainment of this purpose by raising continually the standards of requirement for successful examination on the part of applicants for license to practice.

In the special domain of surgery the state can point to many able and even brilliant practitioners. Every community has one or more skillful surgeons, and the wonderful possibilities to which the door was opened by the advent of antiseptic surgery and its finer development, aseptic surgery, are fully realized in West Virginia in 1913.

The light through which must be viewed the beginnings of all activities in West Virginia is blurred by the reek of war. Enough is seen clearly, however, to permit a fair judgment concerning our growth and progress. Great as are the changes and advances that the state has witnessed within its confines during the fifty years of its life, there is none in any field of human endeavor that is more noteworthy and more vital than the development of medical practice and public health.

WEST VIRGINIA: AGRICULTURE AND
NATURAL RESOURCES

This article illustrates the condition of the state's agriculture and natural resources at the beginning of the second decade of the 20th Century.

Source: Joe Mitchell Chapple. West Virginia. The Land Overlooked. Reprinted from the National Magazine, December 1913. Published by the Department of Agriculture, State of West Virginia, 1-16.

West Virginia ❧
The Land Overlooked
by Joe Mitchell Chapple

SETTLED between the eras of colonial development and the subsiding rush to the Middle and Far West, West Virginia, long "the land overlooked," is today the land of promise. The wonders of West Virginia have in years past furnished a background for many a thrilling romance, but now this young state, which has just celebrated its fiftieth birthday, is taking its place in the front rank of American commonwealths.

West Virginia has more variety of climate, latitude and longitude considered, than has any other state. The last census registered a greater proportion of American born people living in West Virginia than in any other state. It has more blue grass territory than Kentucky; more coal than Pennsylvania and Ohio combined. Every variety of thermal and non-thermal spring bubbles within its mountainous borders. Since the time when the Indians first discovered their virtues, the White Sulphur Springs of West Virginia have been famous the world over. The trails and "deer licks" or salt springs and wooded hills and watered fields of West Virginia captivated the young surveyor, George Washington, when he made his first exploring trip from home up the South branch of the Potomac when scarcely sixteen years of age. In early manhood he surveyed Romney, nestling in the great Appalachian orchards, and today one of West Virginia's thriving and historic towns. Later in life Washington returned on a military expedition with Braddock through the beautiful West Virginia valleys to attack Fort Duquesne, where today Pittsburgh's skyscrapers and lurid smoke curtain skirt this storied river. The young Virginian, despite the tragic defeat and death of his commander, never forgot the beauty and charm of the scenes he traversed, and his vision of the future is today revealed in the majestic and splendid growth of the youngest state of the east. One of the last battles of the Revolution was fought on West Virginia soil at Point Pleasant. An appropriate monument for the historic spot was later provided for by Congress through the efforts of former Senator Nathan B. Scott, and thus this impressive shaft links West Virginia to the tradition of the thirteen colonies, although the commonwealth was the storm child of the Civil War.

But a movement for the creation of a new state from the Old Dominion began long before the fratricidal struggle. In early days the western part of the state was isolated frontier territory, and the sturdy pioneers had very little voice in the state affairs which the tide water counties controlled. The rift in the historic old colony was perceptible soon after the Revolution, when the sturdy farmers of northwestern Virginia were allowed only one vote against the three given the planters on the east shore of Virginia, and this after a bloody fight against taxation without representation. When the cleavage occurred, a clause in the Constitution provided that the new state should pay a reasonable proportion of state indebtedness according to the benefits accruing to the new state, This question was carried to the Supreme Court, who suggested that West Virginia should liquidate one-third of the state debt, although when the new commonwealth was launched, she did not have a public institution within her borders.

Within the borders of West Virginia have centered great dramas of national life. Her very mountains are bathed in the purple mists of romance, for it was the intersecting point of the great turnpike of trade between the west, north, south and east—the very axis as it were of the wheel of westward migration. The mountain ranges are the natural boundaries of West Virginia, and the curious shape of the state resembles a toad—the legs representing the east and west panhandles of the state, and the head dipping down into Kentucky, along the historic Big Sandy.

When West Virginia was created, with its twenty thousand square miles of coal lands, the Baltimore and Ohio railroad (which carried most of the troops from

West to East during the Civil War) preferred to keep its right-of-way entirely within Federal lines. This request was granted. For this reason the state line dipping into Virginia was made to include Harpers Ferry, where John Brown's raid was made in 1859. Every mile of the Baltimore & Ohio Railroad open in 1857 west of Baltimore was located within the borders of the new Union state created in 1863.

* * *

Following the railroad lines which thread the river levels, one can only begin to realize what an immense territory lies beyond, in the great uplands and valleys. Think of a state in which Randolph County alone contains 2,600 square miles, twice as large as the entire state of Rhode Island! One of the old "Shoe String" Congressional Districts was two hundred miles long, almost like a map of Chile. Until 1885 there were no north and south railroads, thus leaving great stretches of land completely isolated. About this time Hon. Henry Gassoway Davis and the late Senator Stephen B. Elkins began their immense railroad operations, and since 1888 more than fifty or sixty state millionaires have drawn princely fortunes from the natural and logical development of West Virginia.

In traveling over West Virginia today the visitor is amazed at the wealth of natural resources concentrated here, yet overlooked in nearly three centuries of development. The greatest body of hard wood and poplar lumber standing in the country lies within the state. There are more than one hundred thousand farms in West Virginia, an unusual number, considering that the total population is only a million and a quarter people. This does not look as if coal mining in West Virginia was the only industry. For the past two decades, the development of the State has been so great that the railroads in million-dollar expenditures have not been able to keep pace with her needs and deserving. The welcome extended to newcomers has brought in millions of new capital, and the investments keep on accumulating as development is made. The Standard Oil Company in its early years was prominent in the development of the oil fields, furnishing pipe line transportation, and the romance of their development more than repeats that of Pennsylvania.

From the heart of West Virginia, coal is shipped by the acre in large barges down the Kanawha and Ohio rivers. When the Chesapeake & Ohio Railroad was completed in 1872, and the Norfolk

& Western in 1890 in the Pocohontas and New River fields, West Virginia coal supplanted the famous Welsh coal which up to that time had been used almost exclusively by the United States Navy. As the largest producer of natural gas, the largest producer of white sand rock oil, and the largest glass producing country of the world, to say nothing of the pre-eminence of its gigantic clay and iron products, timber and agricultural resources, West Virginia is today a state of boundless possibilities and almost exhaustless resources.

The records at the capitol in Charleston, West Virginia, since December 31, 1862, when Abraham Lincoln signed the act admitting the state to the Union, chronicle marvels of state development unequalled in the history of states. An amendment to the constitution with reference to slavery expressly exempted West Virginia from the effect of Lincoln's Emancipation Proclamation, which appealed to other border states, so that West Virginian slaves were not freed until some time later. The adroit and farseeing statesmanship of Abraham Lincoln was here manifested in his treatment of a great question. In 1863 the majority in Congress that gave Lincoln the needed support came from the border states, Maryland, Kentucky, Delaware, Missouri and West Virginia. In the Reconstruction days the development of West Virginia was necessarily slow, but from Pennsylvania and Ohio and even far western states came the young man, keen, vigorous and ready to labor for her development.

Fifty years of amazing progress in West Virginia gives a new significance to her motto, "*Montani Semper Liberi*," meaning "Mountaineers always freemen." There is something in the environment and in the rugged scenery of the state that gives its people the freedom-loving spirit of the Swiss. The semi-centennial commission appointed by Governor Glasscock through Mr. Stuart F. Reed, now Secretary of State, made an astounding showing of what this young state has accomplished in five decades. State pride in West Virginia was awakened by this event, and Mr. Reed designed a map that reveals at a glance in a most startling and graphic way the strategic importance of West Virginia as compared with any other state of the Union. A circle with a radius of two hundred and fifty-five miles makes West Virginia the center of all the markets laved by the waters of the Atlantic and the Great Lakes to the north. Within this circle is located the capital of the nation and

twelve of the world's great cities.

It has often been stated that West Virginia is the most northern of the southern states and the most southern of the northern states, the most eastern of the western states and the most western of the eastern states. This epigrammatically depicts the incomparable location of the mountain commonwealth.

Threading the mountain slopes and valleys of this state, eighty steam and electric railroads cover over six thousand miles of trackage and show an assessed valuation of two hundred millions of dollars—a snug budget for an infant commonwealth. Four splendid inland rivers, the Big Sandy, Great Kanawha, Little Kanawha and Monongahela, all having modern locks and dams under Uncle Sam's supervision, provide the most economic method of transportation of coal from the very shafts of the mines and the very heart of the state's great natural resources to the markets of the world. Many streams, tributaries to the Ohio, wash her western boundary and sweep on to the great industrial centers of the north, south and middle west. On the north, but a few hours distant, lie the Great Lakes; on the east it is only a hundred miles to tide water. This map is thoroughly impressed upon the mental vision of every scholar in the six thousand schools of West Virginia.

* * *

The year 1707 does not seem so very long ago as a date in Colonial history. It was then that the first white man, John Lederer, located in West Virginia. The Morgan cabin in Berkeley County was built in 1727. The first governor of the state, A. I. Boreman, lived to see it levy the lowest average tax rate of the forty-eight states in the Union. Mere figures are difficult to comprehend, but when one realizes that the assessed wealth of West Virginia in 1912 was more than a billion dollars, with a state tax of only two and one-half cents on one hundred dollars valuation, it looks as if many of the problems of older commonwealths had been solved in distributing the burden of taxation. More than three hundred thousand pupils were enrolled in the West Virginia schools, and with thirty-two thousand miles of turnpikes and country roads, the initiation of the great nation-wide movement for good roads has been actually begun in West Virginia as a statehood proposition. The value of farm products in 1910 was more than $71,000,000, exceeding the value of coal $52,000,000 and of lumber $15,000,000, while oil and gas production crowding close on $31,000,000, rounded out a total of nearly a quarter billion of products. These figures simply show the remarkable aggregate of products obtained in West Virginia and seem like dealing with astronomical calculations.

Even a few days' tour through West Virginia emphasizes the fact that many of the popular estimates of this wonderful young state are erroneous! To think that the reputation of a commonwealth can be determined by the difficulties of adjusting the relations of capital to labor in two small coal creeks is absurd. The real solidity of West Virginia is personified in Governor Hatfield, himself a descendant of sturdy mountaineers, who hails from the southern part of the state, and who with a strong grasp held in check dangerous labor troubles when Federal interference was proposed. Governor Hatfield went among the miners, got his evidence at first-hand, and showed the humanity and fairness needed, soon making employers and employees realize that to obey the law was their best policy. The expense and danger of further military intervention was avoided. As I stood talking to the governor in his office at Charleston, he showed the documentary evidence on which he based those firm and sweeping decisions which brought peace out of chaos.

West Virginians are patriotic. It was West Virginian founders who took the native ore from their mountains and made the cannon balls with which Commodore Perry defeated the British fleet on Lake Erie. In that same battle Captain Elliott, a former Wheeling boy, commanded the Niagara, to which Perry transferred his flag when his own vessel, the Lawrence, was disabled by the British fire and at the mercy of her antagonists. Captain Chadwick, a Morgantown boy, commanded the flagship New York when the Spanish fleet went down at Santiago. Bounded on the north by Pennsylvania, on the west by Ohio and by Virginia, the mother-state, on the east, West Virginia is a natural blend, a composite, as it were, of American initiative and enterprise, and the natural development of the state is only to be compared with the splendid and sturdy development of its citizenship. Think of traversing one county where six million fruit trees are in leaf and blossom! The South Branch orchard country is a revelation in fruit production. The cheap and free lands of the west enabled the railroads to expend a million dollars for advertising in the east with cheap tourist rates to

tempt farmers to go West. Since then the prairies have been converted into wheat and corn fields, the valleys into orchards, and the western states have gained population heavily and steadily at the expense of the East. But today men find conditions that are bringing back some of the wayfaring ones who wandered west. In close proximity to markets, West Virginia fruit growers possess especial advantages over their competitors. Is it any wonder they are going back to find the very climate especially fitted for growing peaches and apples, and other conditions favorable to fruit growers such as do not exist in any other section of the country?

Here one realizes that West Virginia is "The Land Overlooked," for in all parts of the state nature has given with a more lavish hand. Lying east of the Alleghany Range, which acts as a barrier to states from the west—especially the late, cold waves that sweep the plains and valleys of the Middle West in the early springtime—at elevations of from 900 to 2,000 feet above sea level, one finds a soil adapted to all kinds of fruit, especially peaches and apples. No section of the country offers better opportunity for the man with small capital to invest.

In the little town of Romney, the county seat of Hampshire, rich in historical memories; in Moorefield, the county seat of Hardy; and in Petersburg, the county seat of Grant, there are located prosperous wood-working plants, and around them poultry raising and fruit farming have been developed to a greater extent than in almost any other section of the country. In Hardy County lie great iron beds, close to mountains of limestone formation, while a few miles westward the coal fields of the Alleghanies combine to make the production of iron easier and cheaper than in any other place in the world. It is impossible to portray in words the fascination of the South Branch Valley as the train rushes along and reveals prosperous farms, while beyond the purple mountain tops lie mines of inestimable wealth.

The story of the railroad development in West Virginia has all the fascination of a romance of the rail. The records as related by Hon. Henry Gassoway Davis, former United States Senator and candidate for Vice-president, show West Virginia originally an impassable hill and mountain state, unexplored and sparsely settled, but with a people determined to join the world in railroad development.

In early days before there were two Virginias, it was the western part of the state that joined with its neighbor Maryland in assisting in the construction of the first railroad in the New World. The old National Pike which ran between Baltimore, Cumberland, Maryland, Uniontown, Pennsylvania, and Wheeling, West Virginia, was the first method of communication between West Virginia and the eastern coast, freight being hauled by trains of the old Conestoga wagons. The rates for transportation then would make the Interstate Commerce Commissioners nowadays stand aghast.

As far back as 1827 the legislature of Maryland passed an act to incorporate the Baltimore & Ohio Road, which was begun on the 4th of July, 1828, with the Ohio River as the objective terminal point. Consequently the soil of West Virginia was the first to feel the impress of a transcontinental railroad undertaking. Harper's Ferry was reached in 1834, at which time began the great struggle to cross the mountains. Not until 1836 was Wheeling definitely agreed upon as the western terminal, and not until 1852 was the road completed to that point on the Ohio River—making good the name of the railroad, Baltimore & Ohio. The lines united at Roseby Rock on the soil of West Virginia, and the wedding of the Ohio River and the Chesapeake Bay was made the occasion of a great celebration.

As pointed out by Senator Davis, a very small percentage of the traveling public ever stop to consider the difference between the swiftness and convenience of the trains of today and the stagecoach of not many years ago. No one would dream of going from San Francisco to New York in a prairie schooner to keep a business engagement—prairie schooner trips are now a memory of a remote past and the wagons are only found in Wild West shows and museums.

Senator Davis also calls attention to the immense manufacturing possibilities of the state, with its cheap fuel, coal and gas. "New railroads will have to be built," he says, and the cost of building and maintaining a railroad in such a mountainous country as West Virginia requires an immense capital. He insists, however, that capital will be forthcoming when the laws of supply and demand warrant new lines, and this time is not very far distant. As long as the railroads prosper, so will the state, and the reverse of this statement is equally true.

Making good roads in West Virginia no longer depends upon debating societies and "resoluting" conventions. A practical advance toward better highways has been made in West Virginia, so that millions of dollars will be saved on the transportation of products, to say nothing of increased development. The importance of good roads in promoting better health, better schools and better farms, and the fact that unimproved roads are an important cause of the increased cost of living are plainly set forth in West Virginia. Through a system recently installed, giving each county a section of highway to build and maintain, rapid improvement of these highways is assured.

United States Senator W. E. Chilton has made good roads the one great hobby of his life, and already a highway is being constructed through West Virginia that will connect the city of Washington, the scene of Lincoln's immortal achievements, with Harden County, Kentucky, the place of his birth. This will mean good highways across the Alleghenies. What monument could seem more appropriate to the memory of Lincoln?

Although the first telephone line was built in West Virginia in 1879, yet the state today is threaded with a telephone system reaching to its most remote parts. This feature of West Virginia is quite in keeping with the general progress that follows commercial development. West Virginia's first long-distance wire was constructed in 1894, and today, not ten years later, messages from all parts of West Virginia to the commercial and business centers of the world, flash night and day over the wires, thus keeping the isolated mountains in touch with the financial centers of the metropolis.

* * *

In an article recently published by Mr. Roy Benton Naylor, Secretary of the West Virginia Board of Trade, he insists that the best assets of West Virginia are in the commercial organization of the state. The West Virginia Board of Trade has for its object the general advancement of the state, and its membership includes men in all branches of business. Its list of former presidents is a veritable roster of leading West Virginians; Hon. John J. Cornwell, the present president of Romney, has been very active in pushing forward all West Virginian interests. Through the State Board of Trade all organizations of the state work in harmony. They have attracted new enterprises involving the investment of millions of dollars, and have greatly improved railroad facilities. Among associations that have an active civic spirit are: Bluefield Chamber of Commerce; Charleston Chamber of Commerce; Clarksburg Board of Trade; Fairmount Chamber of Commerce; Grafton Board of Trade; Huntington Chamber of Commerce; Keyser Board of Trade; Mannington Board of Trade; Martinsburg Board of Trade; Morgantown Board of Trade; Moundsville Board of Trade; New Martinsville Board of Trade; Parkersburg Board of Commerce; Richwood Board of Trade; St. Albans Board of Trade; Salem Board of Trade; South Branch Board of Trade; Weston Board of Trade; Wheeling Board of Trade; Williamson Board of Trade; West Virginia Live Stock Association; Sheep Breeders' and Wool Growers' Association; Dairy Association; Poultry Association; Horticultural Association, and the West Virginia State Grange.

Besides the general organizations indicated in this list, most of the cities in the state have retail merchants' associations working for the particular interest of the community at large, while at Montgomery, Point Pleasant, Wellsburg, Keystone, Hinton and Elkins these associations are doing the work indicated, which usually falls to the Board of Trade or Chamber of Commerce in any city. An inter-county organization known as the South Branch Board of Trade was organized in 1911, and gives special attention to the great fruit section called "The Land Overlooked." Memberships from the three counties of Hampshire, Hardy and Grant are included in this organization.

On the mountain ridges of West Virginia and along the banks of the mountain streams are thousands of acres of virgin giant oaks, hickory and maples and the famous yellow poplar and black walnut. These giants of the primeval forests have reached maturity undisturbed, furnishing a variety of forest reserve now known in any other eastern state. One authority has stated that the first sawmill built in West Virginia was located in the valley of the Potomac as far back as revolutionary times, but, for a century after, little was done toward the development of the lumber business. Small sawmills have been operated in West Virginia for two hundred years, but there still remain millions of acres of primeval forest. In 1910 over a billion and a half of lumber was cut in West Virginia, which included a production of more chestnut and cherry timber than that of any other state. The forest

industries have brought into the state a large number of wood-working and collateral industries.

In the lumber camps is nurtured the sturdy, self-reliant mountaineer hardiness reflected in the spirit of the state.

Many romantic stories are told as to the discovery of oil. An amusing incident is taken from an ancient record. In 1807, on the Great Kanawha near Charleston, several salt wells were established and there was difficulty in striking the salt. After many vexatious failures one planter left some darkies working at a well, giving them instructions to keep on digging until they "struck salt or reached hell." They kept on digging while the planter went to visit in a neighboring town. Post-haste came one of the darkies, his eyes rolling. "Massey, Massey, we struck it." "You mean you struck salt?" asked the planter. "No," was the reply, "we struck hell, and she am afire with the flames of Lucifer." In digging for salt they had struck gas, which had ignited and formed a vivid conception of the lower regions, according to the darkey conception of the place of torment.

At first the gas was considered a nuisance and the oil was used only for medicine. Later it was used for lamps and workshops. The real value of gas was discovered along the Little Kanawha. A number of Parkersburg men who had abandoned the salt project secured large paying quantities of oil instead, and gas was utilized. The romance incident to all oil developing sections of the country was experienced in West Virginia. Hundreds of thousands of barrels of oil were shipped, floated and rafted to Parkersburg, and from there sent on to market. During the war General Jones of the Confederate Army destroyed about three hundred thousand barrels of oil at Burning Springs. The revival of the oil development came immediately after the war, and in 1872 the start was made toward keeping the statistics. The Fairview Oil Fields were opened in 1890 when the famous "Copeley" well was drilled in Lewis County and opened a new territory in Gordon Sand.

In 1910 nearly twelve million barrels of oil were produced, and with the oil came bubbles of natural gas instead of salt, and when the gas was first used for manufacturing purposes in 1843, it realized a vision of the future which had lain dormant for one half a century.

Since the first colonists migrated to America, the American people have been at heart hunters and anglers. The wild life found on the American continent has furnished a theme for many an entrancing tale, and in these later days when the hostile Indian is no longer in evidence and the needs of the people supplied by the domestic meats, the hunting spirit of the people has lapsed. A century before the big game hunting in the Rocky Mountains, West Virginia was recognized as the great hunting ground of the men of the eastern coast.

Nearly all the large game has been exterminated except the Virginia white-tailed deer and black bear. The mammoth elk of early days has vanished, and the records show that in 1753 the now extinct buffalo were roaming in large herds over the state.

* * *

Some poet has called West Virginia the birthplace of rivers which find their source in the lofty mountain peaks and wind their way through the forests to the Atlantic Ocean on one side and the Gulf of Mexico on the other. One thing for which West Virginia is noted in modern geography is its navigable rivers. In traveling through the mountains one can find hundreds of species of fish in the streams and lakes, and the scenery in these regions surpasses even the entrancing beauty of Switzerland. Is it any wonder that the West Virginian takes pride in his home state as an ideal vacation ground?

In the early days of the republic many a sturdy colony started to find homes in the new lands west of the Alleghenies. Among them there were but few who stopped in West Virginia, for it was remote from the regular turnpike and the intrepid spirit of pushing on and on under the magnetic spell of the western sun was irresistible.

Agriculture as shown by recent statistics is the one great resource of the state for present and future development. In one district of the state alone nearly six million fruit trees are ready to blossom next year. Thrifty farm development has taken place along the fertile lands of Moorefield, while the blue grass lands of Greenbrier and Monroe Counties have become famous for their high-class saddle and driving horses and their short-horned cattle. Of the fifteen million acres of land in West Virginia there are only about five million that can be put under the plow, and five million more that can be plowed but very little, being used for orchards and pasturage, which leaves about five million that cannot be

profitably used for farm cultivation. West Virginia has more broken surface than any state in the Union, with elevations reaching from three hundred feet to five thousand feet, and the great variety of soil to be found in a virgin state which is always fertile is the basis for the belief that a million farms will some day be the pride of the state.

The temperature and rainfall in all parts of the state have been thoroughly studied from accurate records and are found to be equally as variable as the surface of the state. The winds blow largely from the southwest, occasionally from the northwest, but very rarely from the east. Cyclones and hurricanes are unknown. The climate is healthful and invigorating. What more can you picture for ideal farm life?

Nearly all kinds of grain, fruits, tobacco and grass have been profitably grown, as the climate is favorable for their cultivation. Up to 1860 nearly eighty per cent of West Virginia's population was on the farms. Agriculture developed from the cradle, scythe and sickle to the modern methods of farming that pay good profits. A steady and substantial increase in farm development is recorded each succeeding year, but the full possibilities of agriculture in West Virginia have not been fully realized until recent years.

Under the direction of Mr. Howard E. Williams of the State Department of Agriculture, and with the Agricultural Department at Washington at hand, the future of West Virginia's agricultural resources will make a showing in the next few years that will be nothing short of startling, for the basis is there for an unparalleled growth. The peach and the apple are the chiefly grown fruits, but plums, grapes, cherries, pears and berries of all kinds grow in lavish quantities. The native wild fruits of West Virginia include blackberries and dewberries, and growing along the glades of Pocahontas and in many other counties are the natural cranberries. The pawpaw and persimmon are native products, and West Virginia knows how to handle the pole to get the persimmon. Despite the tremendous development of the agricultural resources of West Virginia, more than six million dollars' worth of vegetables are imported into the state. This shows something of the extent of the home market offered to the successful farmer. Along the Ohio River are millions of acres of available land suitable for truck-gardening, and in all parts of the state are many hundreds of tomato canneries.

Capital and labor have always been attracted to West Virginia, and many general notions growing out of the fragmentary reports of the recent hearing of the United States Senatorial committee have done a great injustice to the state at large, creating impressions that are entirely erroneous concerning the actual conditions throughout the commonwealth. While there are labor disturbances in small and isolated sections, the state as a whole has furnished a record of what could be done when labor and capital pull together for the common welfare.

Years of prospecting were required to locate the bodies of ore. The West Virginia coal used by the village blacksmith by the side of the road in the early centuries has now become famous the world over as smokeless coal. As far back as 1835 an account of the Appalachian coal fields was published by Dr. S. P. Hildreth of Marietta, Ohio. The production of coal in West Virginia starting with the modest figures of less than half a million tons in 1863, is rapidly approaching the hundred million mark.

The superior quality and variety of West Virginia coal has long been known and conceded in the fuel markets. The production of petroleum and natural gas and coal forces the suggestion that West Virginia is today the "great fuel state" of the Union. The vast measures of her coal fields have long ago attracted the attention of eminent capitalists interested in future development. It was the coal fields of West Virginia that fascinated the late Henry H. Rogers when he built the great tide water railroad from the mountains to the coast at Norfolk at the hazard of losing his entire fortune. The analysis of Pocahontas coals shows that they have the columnar structure, are soft, low in volatile matter, ash and sulphur, and are generally known as "smokeless coals," unexcelled for steam and general fuel purposes and especially prized by naval ships all over the world. The New River coals are of much the same fine quality, and it is only a matter of time when adequate railroad facilities will make the tremendous coal production of West Virginia greater than that of any other state in the nation. These coals, on account of their high fuel value and resistance to pulverization in transportation and handling, as well as their small loss of fuel value in storage, have built up a market for "Kanawha Splint."

In the person of Dr. I. C. White, state geologist, West Virginia has one of the most noted scientists in the country. He seems to have a genius not only for describing, but for accurately locating the various stratas in West Virginia. He is enthusiastic in the tremendous research involved in tracing back to volcanic disturbances and following out the geological formations accurately. He is responsible for the statement that West Virginia contains more bituminous coal than Ohio and Pennsylvania put together, and that Virginia and Maryland might be thrown in for good measure. He points out the fact that three hundred millions of high-grade iron ores are located in the state, to say nothing of an immense amount of limestone unexcelled for its purity. This lime is of a high grade and is used for every purpose for which lime is utilized. Two-fifths of all the natural gas produced in the United States comes from West Virginia.

West Virginia brick clays and shales are beyond comparison, and the beauty of building stones, marble and granite have not begun to be realized. The millions of feet of lumber that still cover the mountains of West Virginia have been looked upon as one of the great bodies of virgin timber remaining. Dr. White has laid especial stress upon the natural resources of climate, soil and landscape in West Virginia. He points out that a state located as this in the very heart of the Appalachian plateau has for years been the strategic point of easy development of all the lands on the Atlantic Coast.

The immense deposits of glass sands have made West Virginia one of the greatest glass manufacturing states in the Union, and this geological formation crops out in other counties where developments have never been made. More varieties of sandstone, especially adapted for building purposes, are found in West Virginia than any other state. These building stones cover a wide area and are becoming very popular in the construction of new public buildings in all parts of the country.

*   *   *

In the history of natural gas development salt wells are shown to be the logical forerunners of the gas and oil development. The lack of efficient labor and of transportation facilities is the only limitation placed on the state's iron, lumber, mineral, industrial and agricultural development. Large quantities of iron ore are found in the counties east of the Alleghenies which, according to Dr. White's prediction, will some day be the source of re-markable development. The quality of West Virginia's petroleum surpasses that of any produced anywhere else in the world. The list of counties producing oil include over a score, to say nothing of the myriad productive gas wells distributed over the state in thirty-three counties.

To talk with Dr. White in Morgantown makes one realize that there is very little information in connection with geological West Virginia that is not at his tongue's end. There is almost nothing in bitumin-ous coal that West Virginia does not possess within her borders. Dr. White has visited every section of the coal measures of West Virginia and has ana-lyzed all of the various products. He believes that the coal fields of the South will soon surpass those of the North, and no one can travel over the coal fields without catching his spirit of enthusiasm.

THRIVING CITIES OF WEST VIRGINIA

The selection indicates many
of the urban centers, the industries and the achievements
at the beginning of the second
decade of the 20th Century.

Source: West Virginia. The Land Overlooked. Reprinted
from the National Magazine, December 1913. Published by the Department of Agriculture, State of
West Virginia, 17-57.

* * *

THE story of West Virginian thrift as told by Hon. John J. Cornwell, former president of the State Board of Trade, at their annual meeting in 1913, summarized in a most interesting way the substantial growth of the state.

"West Virginia, with its coal and lumber and oil and gas, as its chief products, feels a depression or any cessation of business much more promptly and much more acutely than do the states of the great Middle West or of the South, where the wealth is derived almost exclusively from agricultural and horticultural products.

"Nevertheless, while the past twelve months have not constituted a record-breaking business period, taking the country as a whole, for the reason, largely, to which I have referred, West Virginia has gone steadily forward, increasing in wealth and in the volume of business which her industries and her people have been doing.

"The best evidence of the accuracy of this statement lies in the reports and conditions of the banks, state and national. Let us take, first, the national banks of West Virginia. On September 4th, 1912, when the comptroller made his call, there were in West Virginia 111 national banks, with total resources of $80,951,794.88. On September 10th of this year, when the call was made, the reports showed that there were 116 national banks, an increase of five in number, with total resources of $88,611,333.00—an increase of about $8,000,000 in total resources.

"But, how about the deposits? That is where the best indication of enlarged and increased prosperity is to be found. On September 4th, 1912, the deposits were $50,840,622, while on September 10th, this year, the deposits in the same banks, including the five new ones, reached the aggregate of $56,404,342—an increase in round numbers of $6,000,000.

TAKE the state banks and the record growth is as good. On June 4th, 1912, all deposits in the state banks aggregate $62,152,835, while on the same date in this year of 1913, the deposits were $68,242,230, an increase of about $7,000,-000. The deposits subject to check, not counting time deposits or demand certificates, increased, in the state banks, from $28,000,000, in round numbers, to $31,000,-000, an increase of about $3,000,000.

"These figures show conclusively that the savings of the people have increased; that the amount of cash or credit for cash, in the state, has increased some $13,000,000 during the past twelve months and the increase in the checking accounts shows that the volume of commerce and general business has likewise had a healthy increase.

"The coal output of 1912, the latest for which complete figures are available, shows a most gratifying growth, the total for the year being in excess of 66,000,000 tons, with a value of more than $62,000,000. The product of natural gas for the year was more than 215,000,000 feet, with a value of over $29,000,000.

"In petroleum, our state in 1912 produced 12,128,962 barrels, with a value of $19,927,721, an increase of more than one per cent over the previous year.

"There was cut and manufactured in the state, during 1913, 1,318,732,000 feet of lumber, which output was about up to the average during the past five years, despite the inroads that have been made upon our forests.

SO much for the natural resources and their output. The agricultural production, which in this state has seriously lagged, shows some increase, not, however, sufficient to boast of. The chief interest in agricultural products and in the value of the output of the farms has been in fruit; and this, so far, has largely been confined to the eastern panhandle or the counties lying east of the Alleghany Mountains. There has, however, been considerable planting of fruit trees in other and untried sections, but too recent for any practical results."

A VERITABLE battery of facts and figures confronts one traveling about West Virginia. The people of the state are proud of what they possess and they know their lesson. Schoolboys stand up in a class in school and recite statistics concerning West Virginia. They know that they have one hundred thousand farms and that there is room for several hundred thousand more. They also know that there are fifteen millions of acres yet to be developed; that the value of the farm property approaches four hundred million dollars, to which the land value adds another two hundred million.

The average farm of the state is one hundred and three acres, the value of each farm is $3,255, and the average value of land $20 per acre. What more could a prospective farmer wish to know?

This state is already twenty-eighth in population among the states and territories of the United States. It is only fifty years old and started on its own hook without a state institution of any kind; its development is a worthy monument to the energy and thrift of West Virginians. The state institutions today include the handsome State House at Charleston, which cost one and a quarter million dollars. There is also a Capitol Annex Building and a Governor's residence worth more than a hundred and fifty thousand dollars. The splendid West Virginia University at Morgantown represents a cost of over a million dollars. There are preparatory branches of the University, at Keyser and Montgomery, State Normal Schools at

Huntington, Fairmont, West Liberty, Athens, Shepherdstown and Glenville. From this one can fully understand why West Virginian teachers are in great demand in all parts of the country.

The State Agricultural Experiment Station in Morgantown, established in 1888, has been a potential factor in the development of the state. There is a School for the Deaf and Blind at Romney, representing a quarter of a million dollars' investment. The West Virginia Colored Institutes at Charleston and Bluefield cover a cost of about a half million dollars more. Industrial homes, asylums for the insane, Miners' Hospitals at Welch, McKendree and Fairmont and a Children's Home at Elkins, an Orphans' Home in Cabell County and a Tuberculosis Sanitarium in Preston County show the treatment given to unfortunates in West Virginia.

Although at the time of the Civil War the population was sparse, yet West Virginia in 1861 furnished thirty-six thousand soldiers for the Union and many Confederate veterans. The sturdy mountain spirit of the West Virginians of those days is now incarnated in its development of peaceful prosperity. It has the sturdy valor and courage associated with the Swiss and other mountain countries.

WHEN the millions of fruit trees in West Virginia are in bloom on the mountains and in the valleys it presents a scene that would inspire anyone with poetic fancy. Over the twenty-six miles of narrow gauge railroad called the Twin Mountain & Potomac has been opened one of the largest and most promising fruit areas in the world. Along this line of road from Keyser to the village of Twin Mountain in the valley some of the most extensive and comprehensive orchard plantations in the country are already developing. Located on Twin Mountain the orchards cover about fifteen hundred acres, with an undulation between the mountains, and on a plateau of "chert" soil, which is extraordinary in its appearance and very limited in area. It is a layer of flinty limestone known as Heidelberg limestone, bedded in a chocolate colored loamy soil, the result of many years of rotting leaves and other vegetable matter filtering through the limestone. When ploughed it is very dark, and this soil affords a blanket protection for the orchard roots like dry farming in the West. This development aggregates a total of more than 88,000 trees, and every detail in the science of raising apples and preparing them for market has been carefully studied.

On one side the descent is precipitous to Patterson Creek. On the other it slopes away gradually. On the top of the mountain the temperature has been observed to be much higher during the winter days than in the valleys. This affords an "air drainage." Everybody hereabouts knows the story of apples through and through. In the valley is located a town surrounded by 7,500 acres of continuous and unexcelled orchard lands. On these plateaus the elevation of 2,500 feet affords a well-tempered climate, and the vegetation is retarded in the spring so that the danger of frost after early budding is averted. The land was cleared, a saw mill built, and the expectation of seeing these Twin Mountains covered with trees bearing fruit is soon to be realized, for next year the first fruitage of these large plantations will be marketed. About the same proportion of apple and peach trees are planted each year, but the peach trees of course, after five or six years, begin to bear fruit, much earlier than the apple trees. The railroad company are planning extensive orchard development and the establishment of canning factories to utilize all the fruit. Operations are planned under the management of Messrs. E. A. and W. P. Russell, both of whom are financially interested in the company and give it concentrated attention.

The pruning and care of the new trees to promote their perfect development is an interesting study, and this great mountain slope covered with trees in spring foliage and flower is a beautiful indication of what the future of West Virginia's fruit production is yet to be. The West Virginia Agricultural Experiment Station is located adjoining the Twin Mountain orchards on land donated by Mr. George T. Leatherman, who has seventeen thousand apple trees growing along the line of the Twin Mountain & Potomac Railroad. The great advantages of the fruit growers of West Virginia in being close to the great market secures them a saving of hundreds of dollars on every carload. It is not generally known that the supply of the apple, the "king of fruits," has fallen off nearly one-half in the last twenty years, owing to the desertion of the old farm orchards and the European demand for American apples, which is constantly increasing.

A trip over the West Virginia fruit sections in the winter time, finding heavy snows on the west side of the mountains and balmy temperatures free from all snow on the east, convinces the traveler how carefully and scientifically the location of these great orchards was studied and planned.

The Newton Pippin from Virginia, that historic apple which was supplied to Queen Victoria all during her reign, flourishes in this region. In fact, eleven varieties of apples, including the Old York Imperial and the Delicious, make this one of the most interesting orchard sections in the country. Corn, oats and garden truck also flourish in the eastern panhandle counties of West Virginia, famous for their unique chert soil. In these orchards are also planted 16,000 peach trees. Who can picture this scene with millions of thousands of apple trees adorning the mountain sides having supplanted the rugged copses and forests of primeval days? There is a fascination in such arcadian scenes that inspires the most matter-of-fact investigator.

The orchards are protected by the State Crop Pest Commission, who have authority to destroy condemned plants and trees. The time is not far distant when West Virginia will be as noted for its apples as Oregon, Washington and other states of the Far West, for the work is not only being developed on a large scale, but the manner and method of marketing is receiving close study before the trees are actually bearing fruit. Mr. R. T. Cunningham and H. L. Heintzelman, citizens of Fairmont, have been largely interested in this orchard culture, and their faith and enthusiasm in this wonderfully beautiful work is infectious, for no one can doubt that in a few years one of the most interesting sights in West Virginia will be the blossoming fruit—the forests of the Twin Mountain district in full fruit or blossom.

AT the land show in Chicago for several years past, West Virginia has created a veritable sensation among agriculturists with her exhibit of apples from the Alleghenies. The state has forged to the front as the area of the largest development of orchards in the country. Companies have been organized operating from one hundred to one thousand acres, and in the past three years more than two million trees have been planted. The growers have been netting handsome profits from their orchards, ranging from $250 to $600 per acre, and the annual crops in West Virginia in 1914 it is believed will exceed two million bushels. This enormous product comes from the famous "Apple Pie Ridge" and in chert lands on the south branch of the Potomac, and within almost a day the apples from the trees find their way into the great markets of the East. The distinctive air drainage which fortifies against killing frost and gives freedom from fungus diseases, makes orcharding in West Virginia one of the most profitable and pleasant phases of agriculture.

Three sprayings are all that are necessary in West Virginia, where four to seven times are required in the West, but the vital point in comparison is that three hundred dollars on a car of apples from the West and two weeks' time hardly compares with seventy-five dollars a car and an outside range of two days' time. Small orchards, purchased from ten dollars to fifty dollars an acre, can be developed without irrigation, and the Wind Sap and York Imperial varieties grow to perfection in all parts of the state.

In the higher altitudes Baldwins and Northern Spies are grown and have the same quality as the product of the New England States. Think of picking apples for four solid months in the year. In other words, one-third of the entire year West Virginia people are picking apples from their trees.

WITHIN the past decade the Baltimore & Ohio Railroad have done more for West Virginia, in the way of exploiting her resources through the printed page, than is sometimes realized by the residents of the state. A day does not pass that a new booklet or printed matter is not distributed, calling attention to the wonderful opportunities offered in the agricultural possibilities of West Virginia. Under the administration of Mr. Daniel Willard, this policy has been emphasized. Year after year the opportunity for safe and profitable investment for surplus capital has been pointed out. More especially has the railroad been interested in the agricultural development and in bringing new farmers and new citizens to the state to develop the farmers. Farmers are needed and it is insisted that ten farmers are required for every one smoke-stack of a new industry secured. The officials of the railroad have interested themselves personally in exploiting the state, and in creating new homes. Figures, marvelous as they are, iterated and reiterated, furnish no adequate conception of the wonderful natural resources of the state. The deposits of clay, lime and cement materials, together with the coal and natural gas and building stone, furnish a livelihood for millions of new citizens every year.

The magnificent hydro-electric development of West Virginia is estimated at one million horse-power, and the thousand-foot dam, seventy feet high, on the Cheat River at Morgantown, tells a marvelous story of industrial development. Over a million and a half acres of virgin forest are still standing in West Virginia, and for many years these forests have been one of the principal resources of wealth in the state. Nearly a hundred band saw mills and a thousand portable saw mills are operating in the state, to a total capacity of a million and a half feet. One curious mathematician has figured it out that enough lumber is produced in the state every year to build a board walk, two hundred feet wide, around the twelve hundred miles of the state's boundary line.

An army of nearly as many men as were in a standing army of the United States some years ago, earning over sixteen millions a year, are employed in the lumber industry alone. The decade between nineteen hundred and nineteen ten is a brilliant history of state development. In this brief period railroad mileage within the state has expanded more than a thousand miles. Coal mines have trebled their production, and the deposits in the banks have increased at the same ratio.

There is always a fascination in the superlative and when you say "largest pottery," "largest glass factory," "largest drug and extract establishment," "largest stogie manufacturing department," "largest independent tin mill in the world" and "largest axe factory in the world," this is a resounding list of superlatives, not only in quantity but in quality, that tells a story which no rhetoric could adequately portray. Through the mountains of West Virginia, over the railroads of the state, surges a ceaseless stream of traffic. East and west and along these arteries of traffic are located many thriving industrial centers, and the record of the thirteenth census showing the percentage of increase is but another indication of thrift and development. To show the broad spirit of the railroads, we find in their folders mention of competing lines and of resorts and towns on other lines, and even a most appreciative and comprehensive description of water transportation, covering over seven hundred miles in West Virginia. The railroads in the state—the Baltimore & Ohio, Chesapeake & Ohio, Norfolk & Western, Wabash, Virginia, Coal & Coke, Western Maryland, Kanawha & Michigan —all operate through trains, to say nothing of the service furnished by twenty local lines which tap the great Trunk Line System.

Farmers in West Virginia are specializing, and live stock in the mountaineer state has reached a valuation of nearly fifty millions in the present year. The rich, blue-grass sod and streams of water make pastures that have given West Virginia a distinction as one of the largest grazing states in the East. The mild winters, affording pasturage for nine months of the year, make live-stock raising especially profitable, and the finest of export beef is shipped direct to foreign markets without feeding any grain whatever. With the live stock has come the development of large dairy interests which, with the tremendous increase of population, has proven very profitable. Butter and eggs and poultry, produced so close to the large markets of the East, necessarily command a greater profit for the farmers than in states more isolated and further from the large consuming market.

Coincident with farm development has been the market gardening. Under the direction of the West Virginia Agricultural Experiment Station, statistics have been gathered showing that nearly forty million dollars' worth of products, from the gardens raised in West Virginia, have been imported into the state to meet the demands of the large industrial centers. Of this amount, more than six millions were made up of fresh and canned vegetables. One of the smallest counties in the state has now twenty-two tomato canneries, where over two hundred carloads of tomatoes are canned every year. Tomatoes have been found to be a splendid crop to raise while the young orchard is maturing. Tobacco has long been a regular crop in West Virginia and is now being more intensively developed than ever before.

The welfare of all the people of the state is well understood by the railroads in their aggressive work to bring from other sections of the country the settlers who have been following the tides of emigration to the West. The ebb of this tide is now apparent in the hundreds of people coming on from the West to make their homes in West Virginia, believing that opportunity closer to older settled sections and on cheaper lands is greater than that which, in years past, has lured the stream of emigration to the West.

MILLIONS of dollars are expended every year by Americans in going abroad to "take the cure" or "kur," as it is called in Germany when applied to mineral water. After visiting Carlsbad, Vichy, Aix-la-Bain, Leamington Spa, Bath, England, and many other famous European resorts, I was amazed to find in West Virginia at White Sulphur Springs a real European cure offered—without going to Europe. For years White Sulphur Springs has been one of the most popular of American mineral resorts. Its early history is associated with Indian legendry, and authentic records have been preserved showing that "kur" treatment was begun here as early as 1778. For more than a century this popular health resort, reached for many years by coach and four over the mountains, and later by the C. & O. Railroad, has maintained its reputation and has been endorsed by the highest medical authorities. Although located on the border of the two Virginias at the summit of the Alleghenies and at an altitude of two thousand feet, yet the springs are as accessible and convenient as any industrial center. What a delight it was to find upon arrival one beautiful autumn day that the Old White Sulphur Springs were still pouring out from the side of the mountain clear and tasteful water at a temperature of sixty degrees. Besides the water of the Sulphur Springs there is also that of the Alum Spring, of a widely different nature.

The radio-activity of White Sulphur Springs water is regarded as superior to that of many famous European springs. Radium treatment is given in all of its forms, and the new bath establishment is as complete and luxurious as any of its kind in Europe. There are tanks ingeniously arranged so that exact quantities of carbonic acid gas can be furnished in a bath, as at Nauheim. It would seem as if every kind of Bath was possible at White Sulphur Springs, reaching back to the time of Caracalla in ancient Rome, with a suggestion of Turkish, Russian and modern electric baths of every known description. There are swimming pools and gymnasiums, Zander apparatus, emanatorium and inhalatoriums used especially for catarrhal troubles, with walks, drives, bridle paths, golf and tennis grounds—in fact nothing could be wished for that is not provided at White Sulphur Springs. The handsome new hotel called the Green Brier is managed by Mr. Fred Sterry, a leading American hotel manager, who for many years was in charge of the Poinciana Hotel at Palm Beach, and he is also manager of the Hotel Plaza in New York and of the Copley Square Hotel in Boston. The Green Brier Hotel is done in Georgian architecture, and is a triumph of modern hotel building; in contrast to it is "The White," with spacious, colonial columns, recalling antebellum days and old-fashioned Virginian hospitality.

The world-wide and traditional fame of White Sulphur Springs does not dim the fame of other springs located in West Virginia. There are the famous Berkeley Springs in Morgan County, the Red Sulphur Springs in Mercer County, the Salt Sulphur Springs and Old Sweet Sulphur Springs in Monroe County, Capon Springs in Hampshire County, Webster Springs in Webster County, and the Shannondale Springs in Jefferson County. In perusing a description of these springs, old Nick himself would be delighted to know that there was such an ample supply of sulphur left on earth. Almost every known kind of spring water beneficial to the human system has been found in West Virginia, though they are not all Sulphur Springs. Many enthusiastic West Virginians predict in a vision of the future of the state that West Virginia will become the Switzerland of the Alleghenies, and afford a rest and recreation retreat unexcelled and easy of access. Side by side, pleasure resorts and agricultural development proceed hand in hand.

WEST VIRGINIA, 1863-1913

The following poem by Herbert
Putnam indicates his views of
the state's development.

Source: Herbert Putnam, "West Virginia, 1863-1913," in
    James Morton Callahan. Semi Centennial History of
West Virginia With Special Articles on Development
and Resources. Published by the Semi-Centennial
Commission of West Virginia, 1913, 258-261.

West Virginia

1863-1913

By

Herbert Putnam.

A favored land,--
Secured against Atlantic's chill blast
By Allegheny's steadfast mountain crest,
It slopes, through hill and dale and meadow
        vast,
To where a noble river on the west
        Laves a low strand.

        Its bosom deep
Garners rich store of Nature's wealth for man,
Sufficient for a generation yet unborn,
And generations still beyond, until the span
Of centuries shall reach their utmost morn
        And final sleep.

        Its shaggy hills
Bear forests lavish to his further needs
For warmth, for light, for shelter and for
        rest,
And copious streams encourage its broad meads
To yield obedient crops, at the behest
        Of him who tills.

        To such a land,
Awaiting yet the quickening touch of man,
Came hardy pioneer with axe and spade,
And hewed a pathway for the eager van
Of hard settlers, who foundations laid
        Divinely planned.

        High-hearted he,
As one who bears all upon his back:
With sinews firm, eye keen, and in his soul
Some portent that our present day may lack--
Some vision that the future may unroll
        In majesty.

        But not in peace
Nor solely with the arts that peace affords
Was he allowed fulfillment of his task;
Assailed by foreign foe, by savage hordes.
'Twas only by his gun and powder flask
        He won release.

        Not in the gaze
Of multitudes applauding, did he fight,
But lonely, 'mid a sullen wilderness,
Exchanging desperate day for treacherous
        night,
His hope no hero's grave, his aim still less
        A hero's praise.

        At last he won,
And found his toil's fruition in the sight
Of tranquil farms, by tranquil labor earned,
Low-weighted orchards, grazing herds, and
        fields alight
With golden grain, and willing sod upturned
        To a glad sun.

        And busy mill
That harnesses a torrent in its course,
Then lets it go rejoicing on its way--
Its service fit accomplished, yet its force
No whit abated, eager till it may
        Still other tasks fulfill.

        And hamlets rise
To towns, and towns to cities' teeming marts,
And cheerful homes, and every glad resource
For trade, for truth, for justice, and the
        arts
That sweeten and enrich man's intercourse
        And stir his enterprise.

. . . .

        And still there lacked
The consummation of a civic life;
Authority to manage its affairs
Free from all outside mandate, from the strife
Of interests conflicting with its cares,
        Or grudging act.

For not a state,
Nor independent in her choice of law and deed,
Was West Virginia yet, but subject still
To a dominion foreign to her need,
Her aims misunderstood, her will
        subordinate.

        But never yet
        Did Providence intend such thralldom
    to endure,
Or that communities in spirit variant,
Divided by a mountain chain secure,
Should find that chain a shackle, a restraint
        By Nature set.

        There came a day
When Fate decreed profounder issues still,
Issues that rent not mere opinion but men's
        souls,
Dividing kin from kin, and friend from friend,
        until
'Neath hostile ensigns each his faith enrolls
        In War's fierce fray.

        Undreamed,
The conflict then, ere either might prevail,
And many a toll Death took with ruthless hand,
And many a hearth lay waste without avail,
And many a head was bowed, before the land
        Emerged, redeemed.

        But when it did,
It held a nation newly purified,
        Of passion rid.
A people newly welded into one--
By common heritage of anguish borne--
        By common pride
In Faith well kept, in Duty nobly done;
If more enduring in the cause that won,
    No less heroic in the cause that died:
        And, last, by equal share
In every boon the future might contain
For a great land returned to peaceful ways,
A land no more by discord rent in twain,
But free to choose the exit of its days--
And, confident in union, free to dare
Such destined ills as Fate must needs ordain.

. . . .

        We, intimate
Participants in all this hope, as in the strife
And woe preceding, we found one boon more;

For from that womb of woe there sprang new
   life--
The free and corporate life, denied before;
And West Virginia then, baptized in war,
Proclaimed by trumpet peal and cannon roar,
      Uprose at last, a State!

         Achieved her great desire,
         She did not hesitate,
         Nor did she wait
The final issue of that contest dire--
Holding aloof until the event should prove
Under which flag discretion safe might move--
But as she stood, blood-soaked, and bathed
   in fire,
         With ancient faith elate,
She chose her ensign, and high upward flung
   Her gage--a star--to join the cluster which
      still hung
         To Union dedicate.

. . . .

         Today we celebrate
The ripe achievements of our fifty years:--
         The mastery
Of forest, field and mine, the mill which rears
Its bulk o'er many a stream, the forge and
   factory's
         Incessant hum.
The railways linking mart to mart and home
   to home,
The growth of trade in each emporium,
And other wealth material that has come
         To bless
Our subjugation of a wilderness,
And mien undaunted in a time of stress:--
         All these we proudly sum.
The pride is just; but let it not ignore
Our progress in the things that count for
   more
         In strengthening a state
         Than wealth material won.
         Let it relate what we have done
To further Education, and promote
An understanding near of things remote.
         What may we claim
Of those fine civic traits which earn the name
         Of a great commonwealth.
And are the tokens of sound civic health?--
Respect for law, to each his equal chance,
         For variant opinion, tolerance;
         Yet in the issues real

That touch the common weal
Conscience implacable, that alike defies
The bribe, the threat, or coward compromise.

And most of all,
As we survey the decades since our birth,
And count our present worth.
Let us recall
The hardy virtues that first cleared the ways
To these abundant days;
Nor, in the privilege
Of statehood which has brought us where we
are,
Forget the pledge
Implied when first we set our eager star
Amid the galaxy
That crowns the ensign of a Nation free:

The pledge to keep the star forever pure
By probity of purpose and of deed;
In home and court and office to abjure
The sordid aim, the cloudy arts of greed;
Keep clean and straight
Our private ways; and dedicate
The best that in us lies to serve the State:--
So that the light symbolic of that star,
By us replenished still, shall constant be,
And carry far
The noblest radiance of Democracy.

BASIC FACTS

Capital City .... Charleston
Nickname .... The Mountain State
Flower .... Big Rhododendron
Bird .... Cardinal
Tree .... Sugar Maple
Songs .... *West Virginia, My Home Sweet Home;*
The West Virginia Hills;
and *This Is My West Virginia*
Animal .... Black Bear
Fish .... Brook Trout
Entered the Union .... June 20, 1863

STATISTICS*

Land Area (square miles) 24,070
   Rank in Nation 41st
Population† 1,795,000
   Rank in Nation 34th
   Density per square mile 74.6
Number of Representatives in Congress 4
Capital City .... Charleston
   Population 71,505
   Rank in State 2nd
Largest City .... Huntington
   Population 74,315
Number of Cities over 10,000 Population 15
Number of Counties 55

---

* Based on 1970 census statistics compiled by the Bureau of the Census.
† Estimated by Bureau of the Census for July 1, 1972.

MAP OF CONGRESSIONAL DISTRICTS

OF WEST VIRGINIA

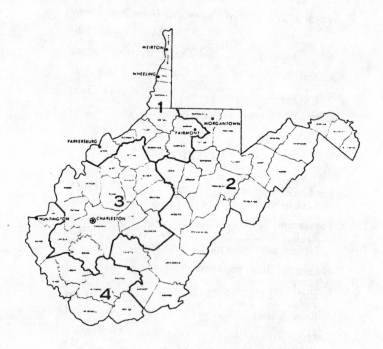

SELECTED BIBLIOGRAPHY

Ambler, Charles Henry. A History of West Virginia. New York: Prentice-Hall, 1933.

Callahan, James Morton. History of West Virginia, Old and New. Chicago and New York: The American Historical Society, Inc., 1923, 3 vols.

Cartmell, Thomas Kemp. Shenandoah Valley Pioneers and Their Descendants. Berryville, Va., 1963.

Cometti, Elizabeth and Summers, Festus P. The Thirty-fifth State: A Documentary History of West Virginia. Morgantown: West Virginia University Library, 1966.

Conley, Philip Mallory. West Virginia, A Brief History of the Mountain States. Charleston, W. Va.: West Virginia Publishing Company, 1940.

Hughes, Josiah. Pioneer West Virginia. Charleston, W. Va.: The Author, 1932.

Lambert, Oscar Doane. West Virginia: Its People and Its Progress. Hopkinsville, Ky.: Historical Record Association, 1959.

Miller, Thomas Condit and Maxwell, H. West Virginia and Its People. New York: Lewis Historical Publishing Company, 1913, 3 vols.

Moore, George Ellis. A Banner in the Hills: West Virginia's Statehood. New York: Appleton-Century-Crofts, 1963.

Myers, Sylvester. Meyers' History of West Virginia. Wheeling: The Wheeling News Lithograph Co., 1915.

Rice, Otis K. The Allegheny Frontier: West Virginia Beginnings, 1730-1830. Lexington: University Press of Kentucky, 1970.

Sutton, John Davison. History of Braxton County and Central West Virginia. Sutton, W. Va., 1919.

Tams, W. P. The Smokeless Coal Fields of West Virginia; A Brief History. Morganton: West Virginia University Library, 1963.

NAME INDEX

Adams, John, 4, 6
Adams, John Quincy,
    8, 9
Atkinson, George W.,
    15

Barbour, Philip Pen-
    dleton, 7
Barron, William W.,
    19
Berkeley, William, 1
Boone, Daniel, 7
Boreman, Arthur I., 11,
    12
Botetourt, Norbonne
    Berkeley, Lord, 2
Braxton, Carter, 6
Brooke, Robert, 3
Brown, John, 9
Burr, Aaron, 7

Cabell, William H.,
    4
Calhoun, John Cald-
    well, 8
Carter, Jimmy, 20
Charles II, King of
    England, 1
Clay, Henry, 9
Cleveland, Grover,
    14
Conley, William G.,
    17
Coolidge, Calvin, 17
Cornwell, John T., 16

Dawson, William O., 15
Doddridge, Philip, 7
Dunmore, Lord, 2

Elizabeth I, Queen of
    England, 8
Elkins, Stephen B., 14

Farnsworth, Daniel
    D. T., 12
Fillmore, Millard, 9
Fleming, Aretas
    Brooks, 14

Gist, Christopher, 1
Glasscock, William E.,
    15
Goff, Nathan, Jr., 13
Gore, Howard M., 17
Grant, Ulysses S., 12

Hancock, John, 7
Harrison, Benjamin, 2
Harrison, Benjamin
    (President), 2, 14
Hardy, Samuel, 2
Harrison, William Hen-
    ry, 2
Hatfield, Henry D.,
    16
Hayes, Rutherford B.,
    13
Holt, Homer A., 17

Jackson, Andrew, 5, 8
Jackson, Jacob B., 14
Jackson, Thomas Jona-
    than "Stonewall,"
    10, 11
Jacob, John Jeremiah,
    13
Jefferson, Thomas, 4
Johnson, Louis A., 18

Kump, Herman G., 17

Lee, Robert E., 10,
    11
Lewis, Charles, 4
Lincoln, Abraham, 11,
    12
Logan, John, 5

Madison, James, 4
Marion, Francis, 6
Marland, William C.,
    18
Marshall, John, 5
Mason, George, 4
Mathews, Henry Mason,
    13
McClellan, George, 10
McCorckle, William A.,
    14
McDowell, James, 9
Meadows, Clarence W.,
    18
Mercer, Hugh, 6
Monroe, James, 3, 7, 8